AI in Application:

An in-depth examination from the legal profession

EDITED BY ALEX DAVIES

Head of events and books
Leah Darbyshire

Commissioning editor
Alex Davies

Editorial assistant
Francesca Ramadan

Published by ARK Group:

UK, Europe and Asia office
5th Floor, 10 Whitechapel High Street
London, E1 8QS
United Kingdom
Tel: +44(0) 207 566 5792
publishing@ark-group.com

North America office
4408 N. Rockwood Drive, Suite 150
Peoria IL 61614
United States
Tel: +1 (309) 495 2853
publishingna@ark-group.com

www.ark-group.com

Layout by Susie Bell, www.f-12.co.uk

Printed by Canon (UK) Ltd, Cockshot Hill, Reigate, RH2 8BF, United Kingdom

ISBN: 978-1-78358-320-1

A catalogue record for this book is available from the British Library

ARK Group is a division of Wilmington plc. The company is registered in England & Wales
with company number 2931372 GB
Registered office: 5th Floor, 10 Whitechapel High Street, London, E1 8QS.
VAT Number: GB 899 3725 51.

Contents

Foreword

Since my book *Robots in Law: How Artificial Intelligence is Transforming Legal Services*, was published at the end of 2016, legal artificial intelligence (AI) has hit the mainstream, in the media, at conferences and events, and in law firms themselves, where innovation, often using AI, is considered a market differentiator.

AI is establishing its position in lawtech, and *AI in Application* brings together practical examples of AI in legal services, highlighting the key offerings and the benefits that it is bringing law firms and corporate legal departments, who are important catalysts for the development and direction of legal technology.

An important development is that firms are fitting AI applications into their technology infrastructure, by combining them with existing resources and integrating them into processes to create portfolio products. In this book, Kate Boyd explains how Australian firm, Allens, created its Real Estate Due Diligence Application (REDDA) using Neota Logic's expert platform, Kira Systems' review and extraction, and HighQ's database functionality to create an end-to-end portfolio product.

Having invested in a machine learning contract analysis solution, it is worth exploring its potential. Sondra Rebenchuk of Kira Systems demonstrates how firms are using Kira for regulatory compliance. Kemp Little has developed a tool to help companies address the regulatory uncertainty around Brexit; Deloitte has created custom provision models for risk assessment to cover changes in financial regulation; and Freshfields Bruckhaus Deringer has trained the system to work in German to enable its healthcare clients comply with changes to German anti-bribery and corruption law. Rebenchuk demonstrates different ways of leveraging an AI technology beyond the defined problem that may have been the rationale for the initial investment, as these tools can be adapted to cover new regulatory challenges.

However, mid-market firms may not have the spare resources or manpower to purchase, customize, train and integrate multiple tools and systems. One option is to design and build a bespoke, scalable solution to address a clearly defined pain point. Peter Bennett describes two of Bates Wells Braithwaite's in-house AI tools: a preventative system for managing the firm's risk, and a document production system that helps the firm deliver on its strategic commercial, regulatory, and social priorities. Although these systems took significant time and effort to develop, benefits have included higher productivity, lower PI premiums, and more effective risk management.

At another mid-market firm, Keoghs, Dene Rowe describes how combining commercial and bespoke solutions have reduced human involvement in high-volume, low-margin work. Keoghs uses iManage RAVN to streamline personal injury insurance disputes through seamless integration between the firm's systems and those of its insurance company clients, enabling straightforward claims to be settled directly. Integration between iManage Extract and the firm's own AI platform enables the firm to continue to create new products that boost its competitive advantage and innovative brand.

Andrew Arruda, CEO and co-founder of ROSS Intelligence, uses several US use cases to flag up the return on investment (ROI) in AI-powered legal research, which boosts profitability by reducing the time and cost of research, as well as democratizing legal services by supporting small firms, and firms that focus on underrepresented groups.

The business advantages of AI tools, in terms of speed, efficiency, and margins, are necessarily shifting the legal services business model, which includes the client side, and legal services procurement. In outlining the rationale and functionality of the Kim legal operations system, Karl Chapman, CEO of Riverview Law, rightly emphasizes the necessity to focus on data quality when working with AI tools, particularly those that involve decision-making. AI is thorough, consistent, and scalable, but its results will be compromised if relevant data or data sets are missing.

AI in Application also includes contributions from legal AI consultants. Richard Tromans, strategic consultant and founder of the Artificial Lawyer website, raises an important issue as he considers the diversity of legal AI, in terms of its functionality, which reflects the range and multiplicity of legal services. Tromans highlights the geographical spread of legal AI, which, unlike other legal technology, has grown into a global movement for change involving every facet of legal services delivery, bringing together legal services providers and start-ups, their clients, and specialist and mainstream vendors to form an international community.

While previous legal technology was often limited by jurisdictional factors, legal AI has become an important transformative element with regional centers of excellence feeding into a worldwide marketplace that is driving progress towards improving legal service delivery and access to justice. The AI tech hype has developed into an innovation movement with a social conscience. Obviously, there will be casualties, in terms of roles, firms, and legacy technology that will be superseded by intelligent automation, and there will be challenges in terms of technology and responsibility, but as this book demonstrates, legal AI has turned out to be way beyond hype – a genuine force for change across the legal services market.

Joanna Goodman, March 2018

Executive summary

There's no doubt that Artificial Intelligence (AI) is a game-changer for the legal profession, much as it will be for the majority of the service industries, in an ever-changing world. Barely a day goes by without the launch of a new start-up, or reports of law firms introducing new AI technology into their practice. But to what extent is AI actually being used in the industry today – and to what effect? Is the much-talked about death of the traditional lawyer any closer? Or is the technology not yet ready to replace the human element?

This book looks further than the hype, and at what actual use cases the technology is being employed in. Using actual examples of AI in practice, the book explores the various innovative technologies being used in the AI sector, covering different practice areas and functions. The intention is that law firms will be able to learn lessons from previous implementations, and consider which technology would be right for them to adopt.

The book opens with a foreword from Joanna Goodman, one of the UK's leading technology journalists, who explores how AI has developed in the 14 months since the publication of her book, and the trends we can expect to continue.

One of those trends – using a "portfolio approach" – is discussed in chapter one, which explores how international commercial law firm, Allens, leveraged teamwork to integrate an expert system with customized machine learning and client collaboration tools to deliver a fully transparent client platform to amplify its strengths. Kate Boyd of Kira Systems discusses how combining three different legal tech "off-the-shelf" solutions, the firm's expertise was amplified, essentially leveraging its unique domain knowledge and making the processes of the most experienced lawyers available across the business.

Chapter two, by Peter Bennett, partnership executive officer at Bates Wells Braithwaite, explores the "simple but effective" matter-level risk management system used by all the fee earners at the company on every new matter. Taking between two and three minutes for the fee earner to use, and gaining the highest level of immediate fee-earner compliance, it is now undertaken 100 percent of the time and is estimated to have saved the company £6 million since 2006, and over £1 million in 2016 alone, when PI premiums went down by a further 35 percent.

Chapter three considers how the journey of AI is not the journey of yet another technology – it is a shift of thinking, mindset, engagement, culture, structure, pricing, and business model. Milos Kresojevic, founder of AI.Legal Labs explores how to achieve all that with little to no budget, how to structure (very) good use cases for AI, engage partners and lawyers, and deliver the benefits to the client. AI poses a challenge not only for lawyers but also for technologists. Yet, AI can deliver significant benefits to firms, lawyers and their respective clients, not to mention society at large. In this chapter Milos talks about how to implement AI, structure use cases, measure the benefits and of course enjoy the "AI journey" in the land of law.

Chapter four by Sondra Rebenchuk of Kira Systems looks at how three types of professional services teams have adopted machine learning contract analysis solutions to ensure quick responses to complex regulatory compliance challenges, including accounting standards, anti-bribery legislation, and Brexit.

In the second of his two contributions, Peter Bennett summarizes BWB's "get legal" service, launched in 2015, in chapter five. A suite of tailored, automated legal documents, the system requires an entirely new way of thinking for lawyers as well as new management systems to reward lawyers for the significant investment in time to produce an online automated document. The chapter also provides a review of the market place in automated documents – a fast developing and important market which will have a significant impact on the legal profession.

In chapter six, Andrew Arruda of ROSS Intelligence explains how working with bankruptcy firm, Van Horn Group, ROSS helps lawyers cut down on research time, thereby reducing their costs to clients who are facing financial difficulties. An artificial intelligence platform supporting legal research activities, ROSS Intelligence uses natural language processing and machine learning capabilities to reduce research time, thus making their services accessible to all.

In chapter seven, Dene Rowe, a partner and director of product development at Keoghs, explains how iManage Extract is assisting with Keoghs' AI initiative, focused on the delivery of innovative products to streamline the process of handling insurance disputes.

Karl Chapman of Riverview Law explains in chapter eight how data is pushing the corporate legal department, sometimes against its core instincts, to the center of organizational decision-making, and in its wake fundamentally changing the legal market value chain.

In chapter nine, Richard Tromans sets out how legal AI tech can be used in multiple areas, and illustrates examples of law firms using legal AI to perform different tasks. Richard considers what this means for law firms and lawyers in general, concluding that nearly all parts of a law firm may benefit from AI tech eventually.

The well-known "pyramid" law firm business model arose in the mid-20th century and had its heyday in the 1970s and 1980s. Digital technologies and the internet now make digital leverage more effective than leveraging with people. In chapter 10, Robert Millard of UK-based Cambridge Strategy Group, discusses how many professions have made the transition to business models that are digital and technology-leveraged, and AI, blockchain and other converging digital technologies are proving pivotal to this business model transformation. While many firms are experimenting with a range of specific machine learning applications, the real disruption will occur as a holistic model of "computer aided law" emerges, allowing lawyers to advise clients at a far more sophisticated level than currently possible. This chapter explores what these new business models might be like.

To conclude the book, chapter 11 takes a look at original research carried out by ARK Group in 2018, into trends in the legal AI market. Our survey respondents identified the uses to which they thought AI would be put in the next few years, and the opportunities and blockages that may help or hinder proliferation of the technology. Those brave enough to have already experimented with AI applications share their experiences, concluding this practical and forward-thinking book, offering a glimpse into the law firm of the future.

About the authors

Andrew Arruda is a Canadian entrepreneur and lawyer, and chief exec-utive officer and co-founder of the artificial intelligence company ROSS Intelligence, a leader in the legal technology industry. Andrew speaks internationally on the subjects of AI, legal technology, and entrepreneur-ship, and has been featured in publications such as *The New York Times*, *BBC*, *Wired*, *CNBC*, *CBS*, *Bloomberg*, *Fortune*, *Inc.*, *Forbes*, *TechCrunch*, the *Washington Post*, and the *Financial Times*. A member of the *Forbes* 30 under 30 class of 2017, as well as a 2016 TED speaker, Andrew aims to forever change the way legal services are delivered. Prior to cofounding ROSS Intelligence, he worked at a Toronto litigation boutique and with the Canadian Department of Foreign Affairs, Trade, and Development in Lisbon, Portugal.

Peter Bennett, FCCA, has 30 years' experience as chief profes-sional officer of law firms – the last 12 years as COO of Bates Wells Braithwaite. BWB is a 25 million/260 staff city-based commercial law firm now converted to an ABS. Previous law management was as CEO of two large Barristers Chambers, a national defendant insurance, and a seven-site High Street practice. He has written and lectured exten-sively on risk management and AI in law, and was named as a leading "innovator and disruptor in law" for the *Legal Week* November 2017 Business of Law conference. Peter was commended at the FT European Legal Innovation Awards 2016 for his pioneering initiatives for BWB in matter level risk management and client-facing document automation – "Get Legal" – both examples of practical AI launched in 2006 and 2015 respectively.

Kate Boyd is vice president of marketing at Kira Systems. With more than 20 years' experience working with professional services compa-nies around the world to embed cutting edge technology, she believes the combinations of great teams empowered with great technology opens exciting opportunities for firms of all sizes. Kate lives in Brooklyn where she geeks out over AI, cool tech, live jazz and peanut butter-filled pretzels.

Karl Chapman is CEO of Riverview Law and chairman of the board of Kim Technologies. Riverview Law provides customers with a flexible, customer-focused approach to the provision of legal services, underpinned by talented people, effective processes, scalable technology, and a customer-centric culture. Kim Technologies is a leading edge software company that applies artificial intelligence capabilities to knowledge automation in any sector.

Milos Kresojevic is the founder of AI.Legal Labs, and a thought leader on use of AI in legal industry. From IBM Research Lab, Silicon Valley to Freshfields Bruckhaus Deringer, Milos has contributed to the Law Society's report on "Technology Innovation in Legal Services" and is a regular speaker on AI and Big Law in New York and London. Milos was the winner of the first European LegalTech Hackathon. Milos' major professional experience stems from work in the IBM Research Lab and Silicon Valley on major innovative efforts for blue chip and start-up companies in the financial, insurance, transportation, and software sectors. Milos has an MBA degree from Columbia University and London Business School.

Robert Millard is director of Cambridge Strategy Group (CSG), a virtual management consultancy in the UK that utilizes a sophisticated digital collaboration platform to leverage a network of leading specialists in a variety of areas of business strategy and management. The firm is focused primarily on professional services and other deep knowledge enterprises. Rob is immediate past co-chair of the IBA's Law Firm Management Committee and currently serves on the steering committee of the IBA's "President's task force on the future of legal services". He is based in Cambridge, UK, but his clients span the globe.

Prior to joining Kira Systems, PR and communications lead, **Sondra Rebenchuk** practiced at the law firm Goodmans LLP in Toronto, where she focused on M&A and securities, and later transitioned to strategic communications firm, Longview Communications. She is passionate about the innovation of the practice of law and enjoys sharing stories of how individuals and firms are making remarkable contributions to the industry.

Dene Rowe is a partner, director of product development and sits on the executive board at Keoghs. In this role, Dene is responsible for developing Keoghs' product offering and also takes responsibility for the firm's information technology, from which he leads the innovation in the firm's case management and intelligence systems. Dene's experience in management of many legal, technology, insurance industry, and insurance litigation teams has given him a breadth of experience across all aspects of Keoghs' business areas and services.

Richard Tromans is the founder of Tromans Consulting, which advises lawyers on strategy and innovation, including the adoption of legal AI/automation technology and its business benefits and impact. He has spent over 19 years working in the legal sector, focused on the UK and global legal markets. Richard is also the founder of the global legal AI and new technology site, *Artificial Lawyer* – www.artificiallawyer.com – which was recently recognized as one of the top 50 information sites in the world on artificial intelligence. See www.tromansconsulting.com for more information.

Chapter 1:
Teamwork, expertise, accuracy and collaboration – an award-winning AI combination

By Kate Boyd, vice president of marketing, Kira Systems

Introduction

When people mention AI and the law, the inevitable discussion of replacing lawyers with machines ensues. While a fully automated approach might work for handling a parking ticket or even negotiating the settlements of an amicable divorce, most corporate legal issues require expert involvement. Clients want to work with legal teams they can trust, who deliver value, who are knowledgeable about their issues, and who have the specific legal expertise for the matter at hand.

One benefit of incorporating machine learning into legal service delivery is that it improves with use, training, and refinement. While out-of-the box solutions can deliver immediate efficiency based on general expertise, as practitioners use and train machine learning technology, the solutions become optimized to the unique expertise of the lawyers, their clients, the languages they speak, and the risks they highlight. This is key to helping firms continue to offer differentiated services based on their expertise.

In the course of providing counsel to clients tackling complex business problems, sometimes the best solutions involve combining multiple AI technologies. In some scenarios this will be an immediate solution to meet a client's need – like Freshfields combining Kira and Hot Docs to produce an end-to-end solution to a unique regulatory issue that required quick responses to very specific needs. In other scenarios, the firm may see an opportunity to deliver a longer-term differentiated service.

Joanna Goodman refers to this as the "portfolio approach" to legal products.[1] As the example below demonstrates, these products can have the effect of amplifying the law firms' expertise, essentially leveraging a firm's unique domain knowledge and making the processes of the most experienced lawyers available across the business. For the firm, this enables scalable service delivery. For clients, this means greater speed and more transparency, without sacrificing the quality, expertise, and precision they demand.

Allens, the law firm named by *Chambers Asia Pacific* as the "2017 Australian Law Firm of the Year", launched its Real Estate Due Diligence Application (REDDA) in 2017. REDDA combined three off-the-shelf legal tech solutions with the firm's unique processes, to develop a portfolio product for clients. REDDA delivers all the quality and thoroughness unique to the Allens' review in a fraction of the time. And it keeps getting better.

Allens' real estate due diligence expertise

Allens' partner, Victoria Holthouse, was an important champion of the REDDA project. With more than 20 years' experience, Victoria has personally analyzed thousands of leases in her career. Her practice group has likely analyzed thousands more in that same period. Victoria's clients range from companies looking to build data centers to multinationals negotiating commercial leases, and real estate investment funds looking to ensure they understand the assets they are looking to acquire.

Real estate due diligence involves the comprehensive review of leases and related documents in order to advise clients on potential issues and risks. Over the years, Allens' real estate team has developed a thorough and comprehensive lease review service that gives its clients a competitive edge in negotiations, and in the long-term, helps future-proof their investments.

"It takes a lawyer an average of five to six hours to thoroughly review one lease to identify material considerations that require further investigation," says Victoria. "On a complex real estate transaction, there can be 200 or more leases for review. Traditionally, this work is done by junior lawyers and is a time-consuming process."

This process-driven work is undertaken in an increasingly competitive market, requiring efficient and cost-effective delivery of high quality and high volume work in short timeframes.

Victoria continues: "REDDA addresses a pain point identified by our clients – too much professional time spent on reviewing large volumes of data."

With a well-documented process, clear review criteria and examples, and an appetite to find efficiency, the real estate due diligence process at Allens seemed ripe for disruption.

Innovation starts with teamwork

Beth Patterson, Allens' chief legal and technology services officer, and her team are responsible for understanding and adopting practice technology to help Allens deliver excellent and differentiated solutions across the region.

The first step for the REDDA project was to assemble a team of experts. Both Victoria and Beth credit teamwork as one of the critical factors in their success. With support across the organization, they were able to put together a multidisciplinary team to capture more than 20 years of legal knowledge into a tool that analyzes leases and flags material issues in 30 to 50 percent less time.

The team included partners, associates, knowledge management experts, technologists and consultants from Neota Logic, creators of an AI-driven platform for the intelligent automation of expertise, documents, and business processes, who from start to finish made it a priority to emphasize the group's strengths and make sure everyone was given the right level of responsibility and recognition. On a project that pushes so many boundaries, it was critical to keep teamwork at the heart of the program.

Automating expertise

The team's first milestone was to map out the process for automating the risk analysis. REDDA is a good fit for Neota Logic because the firm had a very well-established, albeit manual, process for its entire risk assessment program. Working first with process maps, decision trees and a well-developed precedent, Beth and Victoria's team, working with the Neota Logic team, built an expert system that encoded 790 questions in 64 forms with over 1,200 logic items, which Neota Logic still says is one of the most complex apps it has created. The logic for generating over 60 material issues based on combinations to answers to questions was also encoded.

It's important to know that once experts have built the lease review application, the engine in Neota Logic ensures that no lawyer or client would ever have to answer all 790 questions. The guided, intuitive nature of the app increases efficiency at all levels of legal experience as the system guides reviewers through the quickest path, with only the questions being asked that are relevant to the previous answers given.

The Neota Logic component of REDDA significantly reduced the time needed for a lawyer to review a lease and automatically produced the lease review, material issues, and request for information reports.

Extracting the key information

With the logic behind the expert system of REDDA fully documented and built, Beth's team began to formalize what data needed to be extracted from each lease, and in what format, to feed into the Neota Logic reasoning engine in a combined way to get accurate material issues flags. Her team now turned their attention to Kira. Beth's team had been working with Kira's out-of-the-box provision models for several months at this point, but to further refine the data pulled from the leases, the team needed to train custom models. In order to provide a thorough review, REDDA needed to extract 60 provisions from the lease set. These extractions included dates, parties, termination, and other risk-related clauses.

Once the required provisions were identified, the next step was to compile a varied set of examples to train the extraction model. The team knew that the more variety Kira was exposed to during training, the better tuned the machine learning models would be when there was variety in a client's leases. Training Kira required the associates who normally ran the review processes to highlight the provisions used to train the models. While this seems like an unusual time commitment for work that isn't delivered directly to a client, the team knew that once the high-accuracy models were trained for the firm, associates would not have to manually review those leases again. The training process also helped the team clarify aspects of the provision identification, which cemented their own understanding of the issues and increased the accuracy of the inputs.

Once the extraction models were trained and complete, all the data for each lease could automatically be entered into a table format for further assessment by experienced lawyers who would review the data to confirm the extraction was completely accurate. Once the review was completed, the Kira API would be used to push the extracted provisions through to the Neota Logic lease review and risk assessment application.

Collaboration to provide increased transparency

The last step of the process was to connect REDDA to HighQ, which Allens had been using for client engagement and collaboration for a number of years. The team knew they would be able to leverage HighQ's database functionality, iSheets, along with document automation and data visualization capabilities, to produce high-quality reports delivered to clients in the most automated and easily accessible online format. They built 35 custom views, which allow legal experts and clients 24/7 direct access to filter and analyze results in real time, instead of having to wait for a full due diligence report. This means quicker access to insights from the data in new ways that help drive business decisions.

REDDA owes much of its success to a collaborative development process, harnessing a multidisciplinary team with a wide range of expertise. Beth says:

"Our approach to innovation is to develop solutions that address clients' needs and make internal processes more efficient. REDDA is the perfect fusion between complex legal knowledge, decision making, and artificial intelligence."

Managing partner, Richard Spurio, also noted:

"At Allens, our clients are at the center of everything we do. I am delighted that our multidisciplinary team have developed a state-of-the-art end-to-end real estate due diligence process that reduces risk while offering our clients value through greater efficiencies.

"The process of working on this innovative project has been a trans-formative one for Allens and our real estate group, adding significant value for our clients. We are proud to have been able to harness our focus on innovation, our drive to help our clients and the smarts of our people, to produce an elegant, efficient solution to a client problem."

The team was recognized for its efforts at the International Legal Technology Association (ILTA) Awards in 2017 by receiving the "Innovative Project of the Year" award for REDDA. The firm recently trained over 40 lawyers to use REDDA, and now regularly handles several lease review projects per month with varying volumes of review. The efficiency is helping get the work completed faster, as well as contrib-uting to better allocation of lawyer time.

Preparing your firm

Portfolio products are not plug-and-play solutions. Their deployment requires much more than signing a software license and an announce-ment. As a business, a law firm needs to assess the strategic implications of delivering a new product offering, bring their legal teams together with technical teams to map content and processes with an understanding of data structures and product capabilities, and allocate time and effort to the marketing and promotion of the new solutions so the firm can realize their long-term benefit.

Dozens of firms are highlighted in Daniel Linna's *Catalog of Law Firm Innovation*[2] for initiatives that leverage technology to amplify their exper-tise and deliver key services and products to their clients. Some of the more compelling case studies in the catalog are the ways in which law firms are beginning to offer full legal products as part of their strategic initiatives. Of the more than 60 programs highlighted in the innovation catalog, more than 40 are leveraging either AI or expert systems.

Point solution legal technology helps firms deliver trusted legal advice with greater speed, completeness of analysis, and transparency for the client. True legal innovation, however, evolves from the preliminary step of purchasing legal technology to deploying sophisticated and integrated solutions that deliver long-term benefits to both clients and the business.

For firms that are looking to take on similar projects, here are some of the key steps to follow:

1. Identify a repeatable problem to be solved;

2. Get buy-in across the firm, from partners to the technology team;

3. Don't underestimate the effort required to do this work – consider beginning with a project that is easy to automate and gives maximum benefit to the firm;

4. Process and logic before data, always;

5. Teamwork is key;

6. Employ an iterative approach and gather client feedback at regular intervals; and

7. Don't give up once the solution is complete. Marketing and promoting the product will help the firm and the team gain recognition for their hard work and provide the results needed to propel the creation of other solutions.

Point solutions help accelerate service delivery in targeted ways. Your team needs to be familiar with them in order to integrate them effectively. By seeking opportunities to combine best-of-breed technology together with unique legal expertise and knowledge, you will be able to deliver truly unique legal product offerings, which deliver the efficiency and value clients seek while retaining the trusted, expert-driven, knowledge-based service only your firm can provide.

References

1. *Robots in Law: How Artificial Intelligence is Transforming Legal Services*, Joanna Goodman, ARK Group, 2016.
2. *Catalog of Law Firm Innovation*: www.legaltechinnovation.com/innovation-catalog/

Chapter 2:
Preventative maintenance – how AI is helping reduce internal risk at Bates Wells Braithwaite

By Peter Bennett, partnership executive officer, Bates Wells Braithwaite

During the first couple of months of 2018 I have participated in round-table discussions on AI in law at the British Academy, the Legal Week Business of Law conference (where I was an "ambassador for innovation and disruption") and a Managing Partner Forum. I also regularly meet with Thomson Reuters, Lexis Nexis, and the CEO of Sysero and attend legal/IT conferences and exhibitions.

Within those forum (aside from those sales people who think using the description AI is like stardust for their product) there is an almost universal consensus that the public and the legal profession's general understanding of AI is somewhere between unhelpful and wrong. Do not think that machines can do anything other than respond to the programming of human beings. However, what has changed is the immense processing power and programming techniques and tools which have become readily available and at low-cost.

My preferred definition of AI is taken from a BBC radio interview with a Professor of Artificial Intelligence, who said it is "anything that removes the need for human intelligence in achieving the desired outcome".

In a recent *Desert Island Discs* on BBC Radio 4, Gary Kasparov, the former world chess champion, spoke of the first time he was beaten by a computer. He said it was not done by artificial intelligence, but by "brute computing force". In any situation with a set of defined rules, the computer will always win. Its ability to understand defined rules and then run through a million or a billion potential scenarios to determine its next "move", is its winning strength.

So, concentrate on ideas that achieve the objective of your firm or its clients, without the need for human intelligence. That does not mean the total removal of human intelligence. Within any process there will be elements where the brute force of the computer will always be more effective than the human. However, once the computer has undertaken much of the heavy lifting and can present a small amount of totally relevant information for decision making, the human can then be 100 percent effective. The human role is best achieved by concentrating upon this distilled core information and then making the ultimate decision.

Matter level risk assessment – an example of AI?

For the user of BWB's system (see below) it is a very simple process. Originally 10, now 20, multiple-choice on-screen questions are answered, each of which has up to five choices or a simple yes/no. For 95 percent of the risk assessments undertaken – generally taking under five minutes – no action is required. The matter has been scored as medium to low risk, in all risk categories, for the person who completed the risk assessment.

Even with 10 questions there are more than 750,000 possible permutations of answers, of which over 1,000 combinations of answers will produce a call for human action because a risk has been identified.

Each answer is given a particular weighting depending upon the risk which is being measured – and the system is simultaneously looking at 10 different risks, each using a different weighting – from professional indemnity to anti-money laundering, reputational to data protection risk.

Those weightings are mathematical, e.g. if your total score from 20 questions is over 40 points for professional indemnity risk, it is classified as PI "danger". That classification (and how it was made up) generate text on score sheets, bespoke advice, signature blocks for required authorization, emails are sent to risk managers, AMLOs, data risk managers, or a meeting of the reputational risk group is called, and that matter will be selected for file review, when that next takes place.

No human intelligence could take the score answers, determine the results for 10 differently weighted risks and ensure every action was taken for one risk assessment, let alone 40,000, as effectively as the computer. The human would be bogged down with detail and boredom as they assess the 95 percent of matters that are low risk and require no action. However, as a human, the experience of concentrating on the five percent identified as danger (about 12 a month) allows for effective management intervention as the graphs below demonstrate.

Two examples indicate why some might think the system has artificial intelligence in the populist version of AI.

We have identified that the greatest risk factor is undertaking work for which the lawyer has no expertise. For that reason we ask many questions which probe this area, one of which is "How many times have you undertaken a similar transaction in the last two years?" However, we are aware that with human nature, some lawyers may claim to have undertaken a similar transaction within the two years, when in fact it was several years ago. Given we have accurate records for every matter undertaken by every lawyer for the last 12 years within the risk management system, I realized that we could plan out that question because the information was already held by the system.

That is where processing power combined with big data can appear to be providing populist artificial intelligence. You can imagine the reaction from the lawyer if the computer responded to the lawyer after answering this question, "You are wrong, the matter you are thinking about was three years, 248 days ago". Our system does not speak (but it could!), and if it did speak the above words, most lawyers would say it must have "artificial intelligence" – but it is just computing power, big data and programming.

Secondly, following an incident, we added a question asking if the value of the estimate on the matter was over £100,000 – taking that as a proxy for a large and complex matter. That led to discussions with our corporate department, which said that such transactions were bread-and-butter for them and was part of their core expertise. Following debate, we agreed with their analysis and so weighted the answers differently, depending upon the department of the lawyer. That means that two lawyers with identical answers will be given different results by the risk system. One may require no action, the second – where they do not routinely deal with large matters – being assessed as danger and requiring special clearance. Is that intelligence?

The system has grown by small increments over 12 years. The same simplicity occurs for the user, but the value extracted from the data has been multiplied many times over. Indeed, such is the complexity of algorithms that even I, as its creator, now struggle to fully understand all of the actions that it generates. However, I do know that it has given great benefit to my firm, and it has universal application to any professional services firm, worldwide. Read on for the details.

A "devastatingly effective" matter risk system – 12 years of evidence

This chapter shows how a very simple system has been effective in managing not only professional indemnity risk, but also the many other regulatory and reputational risks around client work. In 2006, I conceived and installed a simple, but devastatingly effective, matter-level risk management system which is now used by all 150 earners (including for non-legal services) at our firm, on every new matter. It takes two to three minutes for the fee earner to use and has gained the highest level of immediate fee-earner compliance. It is now undertaken 100 percent of the time – without complaint – by the fee earners and partners.

The impact of the system was immediate, long-lasting, and dramatic in reducing the number of reported professional liability incidents and, more importantly, professional indemnity (PI) claims. That led to a dramatic reduction in our PI premium annual costs. We have saved Bates Wells & Braithwaite £6m since 2006 and over £1 million in 2016, when PI premiums reduced by a further 35 percent.

Figure 1 shows what we would have paid, had we kept our 2006 premium rating, and compares that with our actual payments. Figure 2 shows our PI insurance payouts total after the risk management system was introduced in 2006. Figure 3 shows the impact it had on PI claims needing cash reserves/payouts.

The demonstrated benefits of the matter-level risk management system should indicate that this has universal application to any professional services firm in any jurisdiction. It has grown to be effective at managing all the main areas of risk (and compliance), and has developed into a bottom-up management information system of unique power.

The eureka moment

The risk management system was conceived in a "eureka" moment in 2006. Our PI premiums were very high and getting higher, with a spate of recent large claims. The first PI renewal after my arrival as COO was difficult and expensive. That spurred me to read the lawyers' reports prepared for the PI underwriters on every claim the firm had suffered for 15 years. The reports are detailed – about ten pages each – and are factual and unbiased. I suspect I was the only chief officer in any law firm who had ever read these reports in such detail.

As I read each one, a pattern began to clearly emerge of universal high level common risk factors. After reading all 15 years' of reports, I realized that the risk factors established in my mind after reading the first 50 percent had not changed after I had finished reading them all.

Creating the system

The simple multiple choice question screen – originally 10, now 20 multiple-choice questions – isolates the 5 percent of matters that need

BWB PI Premium 2006–16

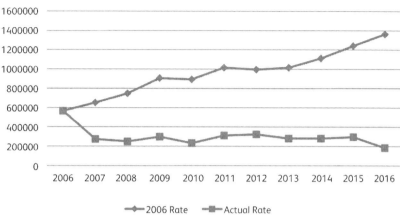

Figure 1: Actual versus 2006 premium rating

PI Insurance payouts £ total

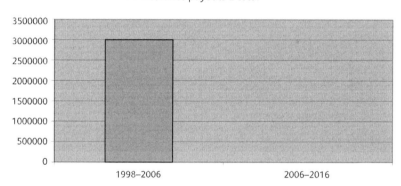

Figure 2: PI payouts after introduction of the risk management system

PI claims needing £ reserves / Payouts by underwriters

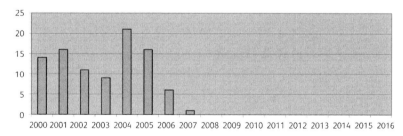

Figure 3: Impact on PI claims needing cash reserves/payouts

real management focus. Just as importantly, it identifies the 95 percent of matters that are routine and low risk which can be dealt with by a light regulatory and management regime.

I was surprised that after nearly 40,000 BWB risk assessments over a ten-year period, danger and high risk matters for general PI risk accounted for only three percent of BWB cases. Carefully managing those three percent was the difference between insurers paying out £3 million over eight years before we introduced matter risk assessment, or paying out nothing in the 12 years since the introduction of matter risk assessment.

A proportionate grading system escalates a matter up the risk management system. At first this was purely driven by a single risk score – no action, one partner signature, two partner signature, email notification prompting a discussion on how risk was going to be managed with the risk manager, and inclusion in the management board risk report. Later, a significant number of single answers would produce a specific and targeted response e.g. we ask for an estimate of the total potential liability of a matter and offer a range with the final option being "over £75 million" which is our current PI cover limit. That option is regularly triggered and brings an immediate case close down.

Expanding the scope

In the past three years, we have further expanded the scope of the matter level risk assessment to cover:

- AML risk;
- reputational risk;
- personal sensitive data;
- market sensitive data;
- newsworthy data;
- potential and managed conflict;
- own interest conflict;
- managing the exceptionally large case (fees over £100k);
- PI liability over £10 million;
- political lobbying activity; and
- financial crime.

All of these are extremely complex areas of risk that are traditionally hard to manage. Once identified as a high risk in each category, a complex set of targeted actions are automatically generated.

Take reputational risk: we proactively prevent any potential brand damage that may come from taking on new clients or matters. The risk management system does not take the decision, but it does isolate the one percent of matters/clients which must be reviewed by our reputational risk group before fee earners are allowed to proceed. Undertaking an in-depth matter risk assessment pre-empts failure and protects the firm's reputation.

Lawyers will not sign an untrue document

The power of the system is that if great care is taken with the question, you will get a true answer. A good example is when we introduced a question on personal sensitive data. We asked partners to sign that they were following a "20-point data security plan" if they answered that the matter being risk assessed contained "personal sensitive data as defined under the Data Protection Act."

In several departments we had uproar, as 70 or 80 percent of all matters required the partner to declare that they were following the 20-point plan, which included, amongst other things, locking paper files away and only taking them out of the office in a locked container. We were asked to water down the question. However, once the partners and lawyers began to discuss the fact that the loss of such files would require reporting to the Office of the Information Commissioner, and it would be a material breach for the SRA, they realized the importance of both identifying high-risk files and protecting them. That 20-point plan had always been known about; the risk management system suddenly made it a reality, and compliance with our systems increased dramatically.

It is the educative power of the risk system that creates the change in attitudes which has transformed risk with BWB and would do so in any firm that used all aspects of the system.

Creating a good risk management culture

The fact that the risk management system isolates a small number of high-risk matters and concentrates upon them, makes practical sense for partners who are engaged in this process. When a matter is assessed as high risk, the partner is required to physically sign a paper which is automatically generated to say that they understand and can manage the risk involved. The pattern of their answers, and sometimes combination of answers, is translated into bespoke advice within the printed risk score. The risk score is read with interest because it distils our expertise in providing advice on the best risk management strategy for that matter. For example, if the risk is being generated by a lack of knowledge/experience of a mid-level lawyer, the advice will be to consider switching the matter to a more suitable/more experienced lawyer.

The next level up from a single partner signature is the requirement to justify your risk management strategy to another partner outside of your department, when a second partner signature is required because of the very high risk of the matter.

The next escalation is a discussion with the risk manager. They receive a copy of the results by email at the same time as the partner score sheet is generated. This allows the experience of the risk manager to be shared with the partner – but only for the highest levels of risk.

Risk-based file review selection is used so that the highest risk matters for every fee earner are selected, whilst danger matters held by a fee earner are automatically file reviewed. The fact that staff know that high risk matters will be file reviewed ensures they are given appropriate priority.

Regular training takes place firm-wide, and within departments, to share with them risk maps of their own department. Discussing a schedule showing the department-specific risks is very effective, as is recounting the pre-2006 big claims against the firm that lie behind each question.

No one element of this process would be sufficient to change the risk culture, but taken together, the reinforcement of understanding where risk comes from, and effective strategies for managing risk, will and has transformed the culture and effective management of risk.

Once the matter level risk system begins to impact on notifications under the professional indemnity policy, reduces claims and makes huge savings in professional indemnity premiums, partners will become enthusiastic supporters for effective risk management.

The second eureka moment

A second eureka moment occurred with the realization that the matter level risk assessment was in effect creating a unique "barcode" for every matter our partners and fee earners handled. Individual scores are permanently attached to a matter and become the equivalent of a product barcode. Once there, it can be read and differently weighted for an infinite number of management, risk, and reporting purposes.

Each PI, money laundering, data, conflict and reputational risk assessment weighs (or ignores) each number of the bar code in a different way, to create its own risk result and consequent risk actions. The list of "danger" matters in each category of risk becomes our firm's core risk register, excellent evidence of risk management for the Solicitors Regulation Authority.

Impact on the firm

We have come a long way since we first adopted risk management strategically. Risk management is now a default discipline at BWB. In fact, it has transformed our culture – unlike previously, and in most traditional law firms, individual partners no longer have the authority to override firm policies. More importantly, partners don't want to supersede policies anymore – the system provides evidence and irrefutable information based on business rationale analysis.

Since implementing our risk management system, we have been able to concentrate all of our efforts on identifying and managing the five percent of genuinely high risk matters. Taken together, the system forces risk management into the day-to-day culture of partners, risk managers, and the management board.

After any incident we review whether the risk assessment questions correctly identified the risk and whether the questions needed adapting. No changes were made for the first five years. However, in the last five years we have slowly adapted the questions and weighting for professional indemnity risk and added new questions relating to other regulatory risk factors.

Twelve years' experience has led to a reduction in the weighting given to the pure size of a transaction and an increase in the questions and weighting given to fee earners operating, intentionally or otherwise, outside their areas of competence.

Adding any new question to the risk questionnaire immediately reveals a whole range of risks that were previously hidden. The risk management system pushes those risks into the knowledge of the central firm management where they can then be managed appropriately.

Lessons for all firms?

From the very beginning, I knew that lawyers acting outside their area of competence were an important risk factor. Many of the changes that we have introduced following incident reviews aimed to identify different the circumstances that tempt lawyers to act outside their areas of competence.

We started with a simple one to five question, where one was core expertise and five was no expertise. We reinforced that with a question asking how many similar transactions they had experienced in the last two years.

Our reviews added, "Is this a service which we promote on our website?" That has picked up lawyers who are about to provide advice that no one in the organization is experienced to provide, let alone themselves or their supervisor.

Next to be added was "Is there any personal involvement from anyone in the firm?" Experienced lawyers' professional judgment can disappear when they are acting for their granny or their boss's granny.

Then came a question of whether the fees totalled over £100,000, including counsel fees. A lawyer may have technical competence on the area of law, but might not have experience of large case management. Adding a reference to counsel fees can be a pointer to a lawyer acknowledging lack of personal expertise, but expecting counsel's advice to mitigate that lack of competence.

Ensuring lawyers (or any other professional services provider) do not act outside their areas of competence is the best way of ensuring you avoid professional indemnity claims. At the beginning of this chapter, I said that the PI claim was one end of a spectrum. A lawyer who operates outside their area of competence will also lead to a badly executed and managed case, which leads to cost overruns, late delivery, fee disputes, complaints, and above all a damaged professional reputation.

Risk, the barcode, and AI

With every matter bar coded as it enters our system (with part of that bar coding the lawyer and following a similar approach to risk assessing/bar coding each client), we are building up the "big data" on which AI can work. Already we compare risk scores with estimates and can give a "too low an estimate for this level of risk" message. We have an estimator tool which loads the price for high risk matters. We could relate the reply to the question, "How busy are you?" back to the estimate – if this fee earner is already at maximum capacity, either switch the work or if only they have the expertise, increase the estimate for this scarce fee earner resource.

Most systems look backwards at events already completed – and that is their limitation. BWB's matter risk assessment acts at the very beginning of the legal process and allows action to be taken to manage potential problems before they occur. At a recent managing partner forum meeting on AI, a hard core maths/engineer specialist linked to Hitachi trains said that in the physical engineering world the big impact of AI is within "preventative maintenance" – using AI to calculate when a system will breakdown and fix it before it does.

We can do the same in law – or I should say, that is what BWB has done over the last 12 years, and the system is increasingly effective and heading deeper into using aspects of AI.

Chapter 3:
AI and Big Law – practical lessons to achieving AI success

By Milos Kresojevic, founder, AI.Legal Labs

The journey of AI is not the journey of yet another technology – it is a shift of thinking, mindset, engagement, culture, structure, resourcing, pricing, business models, and client services. How to achieve all that with little (or no) budget, how to structure (very) good use cases for AI, engage partners and lawyers, and deliver the benefits to the client is no small task. AI poses the challenge not only for lawyers but also technologists. Yet, AI is not only about the challenges, but also about significant benefits to the firm, lawyers, and respective clients, not to mention society at large.

In this chapter we will be talking about how to implement AI, structure the use cases, measure the benefits, and of course enjoy the "AI journey" in the land of law.

AI is not just yet another technology and should not be treated as such for two distinct reasons – scale, and mindset change. Artificial intelligence (machine learning) is a shift of thinking for most of the organization, from IT to information security, as well as lawyers and partners. It is a move from deterministic to probabilistic systems; how one goes about gathering requirements, evaluating systems, and collecting data.

Think big – act small
AI is not incremental improvement technology, it is transformative technology. I call it the "space-shuttle" (or "Falcon Heavy") effect – you would not use a space shuttle to take you from one end of London or New York to another, but you *could*. You want to identify and discover big new bold capabilities for your organization, not just improve existing ones. A good starting point is to think how you would build your organization from the ground up if you had AI as a foundation. What are your largest clients doing? What are their needs? How is AI disrupting them? Secondly, think about your lawyers and partners – the largest,

most complicated matters your lawyers have at hand. What are their big challenges? How are they addressing them? Focus on how AI can help them on the ground, regardless of how big or small that effort might be. The focus should be on value creation for your clients, your lawyers, and the matters they work on – and how AI can help them, here and now.

Adopt an "AI here and now" mantra

Think what you can do with AI now (not once it becomes generally adopted technology). Connect with any effort. Start asking big questions – for every major, big effort, project and client matter – where and how AI can help right now. The answer might be different for different client matters.

You have to decide – consciously and honestly – whether AI is a strategic, marketing, or technology play for your organization. They are all viable and valuable options, but the goals and complexity of AI in an innovation effort are very different. In a case of strategic play, the key question is, "What are the key strategic areas for the firm and what is the firm's competitive advantage?" Your follow up questions should show where and how AI can not only enable and strengthen the strategic areas but, more importantly, potentially deliver bold new capabilities. You may already have started your innovation journey – and you might not know. Those are the isolated individuals (IT/lawyers) playing with the technology already. In order to align, you need to inverse the equation from "Where should/could I use AI?" to rather think "What are the most prominent matters that my firm is dealing with and focusing on?", and reverse the question – "How can AI help my strategic client matters or projects?" Use the benefit of the S-curve crystal ball – when do you want to start exploring the technology?

Senior management blessing is needed (but please, no stakeholder management)

You will need top level blessing to start and support the effort in the first place, but you should not engage in full scale stakeholder management. That should not be your priority and it should not be where you spend your time and effort. Remember, you are running an AI "startup", not a consultancy business. Top level "blessings" will allow you to have full independence from the rest of the organization and shield your efforts from business-as-usual organizational constraints and barriers. At the same time, this will allow you to "play the field" across the organization to develop new AI-enabled capabilities.

Run it as a runaway start-up

You probably assume (and common sense tells you) that a lot of approvals and resources (financial, human, and others) are needed to start on an AI innovation journey. Actually, the truth is quite the opposite; very little is needed. You probably need one or two entrepreneurial staff members (engineers and/or tech savvy lawyers) to start the effort. The focus should be on:

- AI use cases development;
- AI horizon-scanning;
- creation of effective prototypes; and
- finding your first lawyer/partner customer.

In order to start the effort, you have to have an entrepreneurial, start-up mentality – boot-strapping financially, using vendors, open-source technology, and people within and outside the organization to support and be part of your development effort. Your goal should be (1) getting your first functional AI-lite "product" out, and (2) acquiring your first partner/lawyer "customer".

You are in-charge of (running) the start-up in your own firm (which is probably couple of decades or hundreds of years old). That is a challenge and privilege – at the same time.

Horizon scanning – excel at it!

Horizon scanning should be one of your key activities in order to drive use case development and early detection of new, exciting, AI vendors and technology. One key source for your comprehensive set of AI use cases are new AI vendors that you encounter during a horizon scanning exercise. Their AI technology might or might not be directly applicable or of any interest to you and your firm, but their use cases will certainly help you identify additional AI use cases to catalog for your innovation effort. As soon as you learn about a new vendor that might be of interest, engage them early and deeply – to create prototypes, align interest, and create value for both. With earlier engagement it is easier to impact their product roadmap and get their product/services at significantly lower costs.

Use cases are key artifacts

Use cases are one of the key artifacts – they should be high level descriptions in plain legal and English terms of what the inputs and outputs are, the relevant high-level activities, and the ultimate goal of the use case. They should be completely technology-agnostic and when creating them, one should not be concerned about the technological feasibility of achieving them, or their technical or legal complexity. You should catalog them as you go along and they should be the starting point for your prototypes. Sources of your use cases are two-fold – your partners, lawyers and outside parties (e.g. vendors) since their product value proposition is based on one or more use cases. Your primary focus areas are (1) where your organization has significant corpus of knowledge or expertise in (2) the firm's strategic areas (if different from 1), and (3) the major pain points of your current clients' matters.

You should start with three to 10 major use cases, and grow your catalog as your innovation effort progresses. This is a very important point when defining use cases and identifying benefits (not only for clients and internally as well). They need to be big enough and have the potential to deliver significant benefits.

Collaborate (heavily) with AI vendors (use them to the maximum)

With very limited resources at the early stages of your innovation efforts, your AI vendors are your key resource. Most vendors are willing to provide you with their AI products and services at a heavily discounted price (if not for free) and AI legal vendors are in constant search of new legal documents and datasets to build and/or improve their products. This makes your firm's legal documents and legal expertise a highly valuable asset in the AI innovation market. Consider them as part of your team or as an equal partner. Their AI offering, training, and development resources are invaluable for your effort. Treat them as such and take full advantage of extensive use of "collaborative" vendor management. At the same time, your team will become an extended arm of the vendor, helping them position and customize the product to fit best your use cases and your lawyers' needs.

Try to avoid formal, long, marketing-driven vendor selection/evaluation and focus on prototypes and value creation for your lawyers and their clients. Work very closely with them to create the most effective prototype for your client(s), your partners and lawyers. This way, you create value for both organizations. Let the prototypes speak rather than the marketing material. This is the new AI-vendor management ethos – embrace it fully.

Prototype heavily and measure benefits scientifically

There are multiple AI technologies, models, and algorithms that are freely available under open-source license, and while you want to use them to learn, educate, and bring yourself and the team up to speed, your initial development should not be of an AI system from scratch but creating a unique portfolio of AI applications connected and layered up in a smart way that no other organization can replicate. That means using AI vendors to leverage their products and data sets fully while augmenting their functionality with your own development. AI-system augmentation should be your initial focus for software development.

Try to measure benefits as scientifically as possible. In order to properly test your prototypes, you will need a high-quality document set. It is best practice to identify a couple of real-world, historical, representative client matters.

Benefits or benchmarking are very important since they represent hard figures and are the key selling point both internally and externally, providing you and your team credibility and raison d'etre within and outside the organization. Benchmarking should be performed by lawyers or legal professionals who carry out those tasks on a regular basis. Your starting point is large historical matters with historical benchmark information – how long it takes to perform the task manually.

Be aware – you are disrupting your own organization

The fact that you built/developed a successful prototype does not mean your job is done. Your biggest challenge is just starting – how to embed successful prototypes within the organization and align with existing organizational processes from an IT, information security, risk management, and commercial perspective. The time and effort required can never be underestimated. At this point you start to realize you are not only introducing new technology, you are disrupting (basically) your own organization, since AI requires a new approach to risk management, info-security, commercials, marketing, and lawyering of course.

This also creates opportunities to streamline current organizational processes and streamline the organization itself. This is the critical moment on your innovation journey where the question arises as to whether AI is a strategic, marketing, or technological play. It needs to be answered. It is your responsibility to take the wider firm and management on the journey, knowing what the implications are, and what it means for the firm and its business and operating model. At the same time, this means you are becoming a recognizable agent of change (innovation) within the firm. Your natural allies are marketing and business development and client relationship partners, since they are heavily interested in the impact of AI on clients and how AI can benefit the firm's offerings.

Once a new system starts being productionized, the innovation team should hand over production systems to the legal and IT professionals within the organization. However, your job is never ending; you still want to keep an eye on and lead any "innovative", crazy ideas/use cases beyond already implemented ones. For those purposes you probably want to have an experimental portfolio of systems dedicated purely for the innovation team's purposes.

Are you succeeding yet?

Your first signs of success are when (1) your client asks to talk to you or your innovation team, (2) you win client work based on the innovation effort, and/or (3) you get involved directly in the key client matter work and the lawyers and client teams are very enthusiastic of using new AI technology.

At this point, everything from minor to major AI requests will come your way – and you should embrace them. This is the real success – you have more lawyer "customers" than you can handle. You face a different problem – how to manage all those ideas and requests coming your way with your small team. This is the stage when you want to start growing and expanding your team and have all the credentials and track history to ask for resources and proper budget. You became an agent of change within your firm, you are changing the organization, and really innovating from within, organically.

At this point you want to democratize AI across your organization – tell, share, inspire, include, give all your knowledge, and expertise, to the wider firm. You also want to be inclusive of almost everyone who is willing to join or participate or share interest – they become your "extended" innovation team, your ambassadors, your resources and the best people to carry out implicit stakeholder management. At this stage you should already have a special charge code for your lawyers to take time off from their billable work to do innovation work. At this stage innovation starts to be truly embedded in an organization in the mind and bodies of your lawyers, who are enjoying it rather than looking at it as another training or job duty. They become the innovation of the firm. Your role really becomes one of supporting and guiding them.

Finally, the role of innovation is not about AI technology itself, but embedding it into live client matters, the business and operating model of the firm, and offering it to clients measured by the willingness and enthusiasm of partners and lawyers to embrace it and use it in the real, important client work.

With those lessons learned, one should be able to take innovation from ground zero to a couple of live AI systems within 12 to 16 months with real efficiencies ranging between 30 and 70 percent, as well as significant savings to the firm and/or client. However, don't forget – scale matters. Think about big, new, capabilities. And enjoy the AI journey.

Chapter 4:
Easing the pain of regulatory compliance with machine learning

By Sondra Rebenchuk, PR and communications lead, Kira Systems

Introduction

Machine learning contract analysis solutions can help organizations respond quickly and cost-effectively to regulatory changes, such as accounting standards, anti-bribery legislation, and more recently, Brexit. This chapter looks at how three types of professional services teams have adopted Kira to ensure quick responses to complex regulatory compliance challenges.

What is machine learning contract analysis?

Early adopters of machine learning contract analysis in law firms started out using the technology primarily to handle high volume M&A due diligence. Easy to deploy, and often pre-trained by experienced legal knowledge engineers, state-of-the-art technology is able to automatically find key contract provisions even in unstructured and variable contracts, right out-of-the-box.

Machine learning contract review systems, like Kira, are designed to automatically locate user-specified information in contracts, and help spot anomalies to direct human review to the clauses that need closer attention.

To extract key information, like title, parties, date, or change of control and assignment, Kira can review contracts to find any of more than 400 pre-trained concepts, or can run custom-trained models that a firm itself has taught the system.

The text of uploaded documents is scanned, and hits for key provisions are extracted and displayed on the screen in summary charts for user review. Reviewers validate all of the information and can use the platform's interface to quickly review the original documents in detail. Once the review is complete, the lawyer can export summary charts in a variety of different formats for presentation to internal project teams or clients.

With integration directly to data rooms and collaboration platforms, machine learning diligence has rapidly become the new gold standard for law firms of all sizes, from Freshfields, Clifford Chance, Davis Polk, Latham & Watkins to Womble Bond Dickinson, Cassels Brock, and Kemp Little, handling thorough and comprehensive reviews that deliver exceptional client service in less time.

Machine learning for compliance

Firms are now investigating how to leverage machine learning capabilities to go beyond diligence and address regulatory compliance reviews. A number of teams have successfully deployed machine learning solutions to address increasingly complex compliance issues.

Quick responses to regulatory changes require a technology solution that is able to handle both large document volumes and highly complex concepts. Keyword searches and rule-based tools lack the agility needed to accurately respond and anticipate risks in a client's contracts. New machine learning models that identify specific provisions need to be built quickly in order to complete reviews before the regulatory changes come into effect. But the models also need to handle highly complex and variable language, often across languages and structures.

Whether a firm can build its own provision models or is able to access models pre-trained by solution providers, the important task is to identify the probable risks being triggered by the regulatory change. It is critical to have a solution that can quickly and effectively handle the entire population of contracts. Just as no individual wants to hear only half their body has been scanned for cancer, no client wants to hear their external counsel can only review half their contracts.

Large companies commonly have tens of thousands of contracts that require review, a number that is often underestimated before the review begins. Law firms that can provide a complete compliance review, more quickly, and with the same accuracy, will be rewarded with lucrative new business and stronger client relationships.

Uncertain regulations require proactive advice

As UK companies prepare for an uncertain Brexit outcome, and their advisors assemble teams that can provide specialized assistance, it is increasingly difficult for in-house teams to prioritize preparation over other ongoing company business.

In order to determine which of their agreements may be affected or require change in advance of the 2019 Brexit deadline, companies may need to review their entire population of contracts for a number of potential issues, including the enforceability of key provisions.

To help clients anticipate their potential risk exposure, the law firm Kemp Little LLP used Kira to develop a tool to help in-house counsel get ahead of their Brexit-related concerns.

Tania Williams, commercial technology partner at Kemp Little, led the program to identify the critical information in client contracts that required review. With Kira's Quick Study features, Tania's team trained bespoke provision models to identify key clauses that have now become a standard part of the firm's client service program. The training process is intuitive within Kira and is designed to be handled by a lawyer with expertise in legal terminology. No programming skills or machine learning academic credentials are required.

Armed with a faster review process, lawyers at the firm are able to quickly help clients identify which contractual arrangements may be affected by red-flagging specific clauses such as choice of law and jurisdiction. This gives the team the opportunity to proactively provide clients with clear risk assessments of the issues they've uncovered and how they can be remedied.

Tania notes the importance of getting a head start on these reviews:

"It's important for us to help our clients identify these hidden risks now, so they can make any necessary changes to their contractual relationships, and know what issues to keep in mind when entering into agreements going forward."

Using machine learning software, the firm was able to make this otherwise daunting regulatory compliance issue less complicated and burdensome.

Expertise plus machine learning for comprehensive business advice

Providing nimble assistance with compliance reviews is not limited to law firms. As more of the Big Four announce expansion of other legal practice solutions, they are also ramping up their technology-enabled solutions to provide a full spectrum of business advice.

Looking ahead at regulations impacting businesses in the coming year, a number of audit, advisory, and accounting teams are proactively using machine learning solutions to help clients prepare for regulatory changes. These include everything from the lease accounting changes in IFRS 16, to banking regulations in the form of SR14/QFC.

The consequences of the new IFRS 16 lease accounting standard are far reaching. Companies, especially those with complex or high-volume leasing arrangements, must begin planning for these changes well ahead of the 1 January 2019 deadline.

The team at Deloitte LLP is working hard to help its clients stay one step ahead. As early as the summer of 2017, Deloitte used Kira to quickly review thousands of equipment and real property leases for over 40 data points in French and English, using custom-built provision models.

Once the team has reviewed the result of the initial review, Kira can be used to export the results directly into Excel so the experienced audit and advisory teams at Deloitte could provide clients with a detailed risk assessment.

Andrea Taylor, partner and the leader of the legal project solutions team, recently described the issue:

"Many customers do not have the scalable internal resources to complete the review of these leases, or underestimate just how many leases they have to review. We have adopted state-of-the-art technology that allows us to provide efficient, high quality contract review services to clients so that they can focus their resources on higher-value tasks."

Looking inside to find the answers

Sometimes new regulatory rules may be less headline-grabbing, but still pose significant risks and require the help of dedicated, knowledgeable legal professionals to advise quickly.

On a recent matter, Freshfields Bruckhaus Deringer LLP was tasked with reviewing contracts with healthcare professionals and medical facilities for a client in the healthcare sector following a change in German anti-bribery and corruption law. The new law made it an offense, under certain conditions, for healthcare companies to invite professionals to conferences, sponsor training and hospitality, and/or offer payments in relation to observational studies. Freshfields needed to identify any potentially problematic interactions represented in its contracts, and provide a rapid assessment of the client's potential risk.

Given the tight deadline, a document set of over 11,500 contracts, and potential for severe penalties if the deadline was missed, the Freshfields project team, in consultation with the Freshfields' innovation team, used Kira to deliver a cost-effective, thorough, and timely review.

The matter team used Kira's Quick Study feature to teach Kira to automatically recognize and extract the required provisions in German and create the necessary reports for the client. Using analysis visualizations built into the software, Freshfields was also able to see a snapshot of the risk exposure across large numbers of contracts at once, and provide its client with a fast and accurate assessment.

In describing the firm's ability to respond quickly when regulations change, Isabel Parker, director of legal services innovation at Freshfields, noted:

"Kira can be configured around our own custom provisions, using our knowledge base, ensuring that it is perfectly tailored to clients' needs. It complements our own legal expertise, and will further enhance the quality of work delivered to clients while helping to free up the legal services center team to focus on more complex areas of work."

Conclusion

Regulatory changes may impact any number of business functions and require a nimble reaction on the part of companies and their advisors. As corporations scramble to understand how these changes will impact their businesses, professional service teams around the world want to protect their clients by offering advice that is quick, proactive, and actionable. Machine learning contract analysis tools help make this possible by providing cost-effective, transparent, and accurate contract analysis to companies and professionals all over the world.

Chapter 5:
Get Legal – how automated legal documents will change the legal profession

By Peter Bennett, partnership executive officer, Bates Wells Braithwaite

In 2015, Bates Wells & Braithwaite (BWB) launched "Get Legal".[1] It now contains approximately 50 documents that are sold online to clients for between £10 and £200. It also contains a number of free decision tools and a host of useful information for the creation and running of charities, social enterprises, and other not-for-profits. We limited the service to this narrow market because of BWB's dominating brand presence in that market. The assumption was that major players would enter the general commercial marketplace for automated legal document production and eliminate the competition by price. That competition has not happened.

This chapter is in two parts. The first provides an outline of BWB's experience with Get Legal and some of the significant issues that have arisen since 2015. The second provides some background on what is happening within the legal sector on document automation, which should be of interest to anyone interested in legal AI.

Document automation does not fit the populist view of AI as being "a machine learning for itself". However, it does fulfil the definition of "anything that removes the need for human intelligence in achieving your objective".

What is document automation?
Let's start with the basics – what is it? If you consider the evolution of legal document production, it started with the lawyer consulting a range of legal resources to produce freehand advice – probably written with a fountain pen.

Stage two, with the advent of word processing, was standard paragraphs, then boilerplate clauses that could be dropped into your document to save time.

Stage three was the creation of template documents or precedents, which the lawyer would adapt on a freehand basis as they drafted for the specific needs of their clients.

Stage four was the commercialization of precedents, given the expense of maintaining accurate precedents – crucial to their success – and the use of services such as PLC by even the largest commercial firms for their precedent database. PLC now provides many thousands of precedents, maintained by around 1,000 PLC lawyers.

Stage five was the use of mail merge, to enter repetitive data into the precedent before the freehand drafting began. This could be as basic as names and company numbers, which would be merged into the precedent whenever those details were required.

The age of legal document automation

We have now entered stage six – the age of legal document automation.

With precedents, the experienced lawyer would consider a host of information about their client and the legal transaction, to adapt the precedent from being perhaps 50 percent of the final document to 100 percent of their client's need. It probably soon occurred to the experienced user that they were often making a series of choices – sometimes the same sets of choices – to produce perhaps 10 primary versions of that precedent to meet the most common variants of client (perhaps driven by legal form) and the unique transaction. It would have been obvious to that precedent-using lawyer that serious productivity improvements were possible, but for many years the technology did not provide a tool to manage the process or to manage those 10 (perhaps many more) variants of that precedent.

Cheap, simple document automation software then emerged – often embedded in Word. This allowed the software to mimic the thought process of the lawyer. What is the primary information needed to begin to select precedent pathways – employee or contractor? Inside or outside the 1954 Act? Then increasingly detailed questions. This software is a like a river delta where there are multiple choices being offered, each of which can take the automated document down one of a number – even a very large number – of unique alternative routes. In addition to the choice of alternative routes, some questions could remove or add clauses within the current automated document, and some still use the basic mail merge functionality to insert repetitive data.

There are no technological boundaries to the number of primary choices, sub-choices, and mail merge options. That means there are no technological boundaries to the complexity of legal documents that can be produced. One major Scandinavian law firm spent 18 months producing a single automated document process that typically runs to 400 pages in length, produced after hundreds of questions are answered.

The economics of document automation

The above charts the development of legal document automation as a fee earner productivity tool. The use of the Question and Answer (Q&A) format allows a precedent to be converted into a near finished document for partner review by a much more junior lawyer than before, and with the total process being completed at a fraction of the speed and cost of the stage five approach – precedent and partner – which 95 percent of the current legal profession is still using.

For a period, those who embrace full Q&A automation will be able to both win work and boost profit margins. The current cost of producing a bespoke document may be £1,000, with £700 cost and £300 profit. On a Q&A basis the cost may fall to £350 and so the Q&A firm can offer to supply for £900, win the work, and make £550 profit.

Over time, the competition splits between those who continue to charge £1,000 and go bust, and those who automate, whereupon the market price for that document falls as price completion kicks-in.

If a Magic Circle firm, investing heavily in Q&A document automation, can supply for the same price as a mid-sized regional commercial firm, why go to that mid-sized firm for that service? That is particularly the case if the Magic Circle firm (or Deloitte's – see later) guarantees a two-day turnaround whilst the mid-sized regional firm simply says they hope to produce a response in a couple of weeks. Who would you instruct?

BWB's experience of document automation as a fee earner productivity tool

BWB has used its Q&A document automation software to produce suites of documents from within its FCA Compliance (not legal) department. This proved ideal for the production of required new FCA regulatory policies for smaller organizations with simple needs (in so far as FCA Regulations can ever be simple). That was a classic fee earner productivity tool, attracting both simple and complex work to the department. With the Q&A taking care of the boring basics, the professional skills of the department could be directed to adapting the automated document to the complex needs of our major clients.

Rather than being a de-skilling process, it enhanced the professional challenge and interest for the fee earner.

Cost of commercial Q&A precedents?

Before the reader starts thinking that the Q&A precedent approach is totally beyond their competence and/or ability to purchase – continue reading. If you are a current subscriber to Lexis PSL or PLC, you already have access to between 100 and 300 Q&A precedents – for free! Probably many more if you are reading this in a year's time.

Stage seven – cut out the lawyer, let the client answer the question

BWB commenced stage seven of the document automation journey in 2015. This stage is "cutting out the lawyer" and offering automated bespoke legal document production directly to our clients from the Get Legal page on our website.

It took us 18 months to launch Get Legal, due to a host of complex issues that had to be addressed and because of the perception that producing these Get Legal documents was "non-chargeable work", and therefore left at the bottom of a very long list of non-chargeable activities.

Get Legal – a social purpose for BWB

Get Legal was always perceived to be a service that provided both a social purpose and the potential for being financially successful. As an increasingly large and successful commercial law firm, we were aware that many small charities could not afford our fees, but they did need access to high-quality legal documents to fulfil their relatively straightforward legal needs. Get Legal was intended to fulfil that joint purpose.

In order to launch Get Legal, lawyers had to be willing to take a totally new mental approach to offering their expertise to clients. This approach is totally new, novel, and intellectually demanding, even for apparently simple documents. Only some lawyers are able to adjust their method of working and approach to the production of bespoke automated legal documents. PSLs are well suited to the task and may become the "big billers" of the future.

We needed a team of trained paralegals who could take the output of the lawyer and place it within the automated Word entrenched software. We also needed a BD department to help create and market the Get Legal sub-website which contained these complex interrelationships between free web information, credit card sales, and novel automated documents.

Careful thought was required with regard to regulatory and professional issues – this (particularly as it expands) is a legal service being offered by an SRA-regulated ABS. It also needed management commitment and drive over a long period – selling products on the web is not in the traditional skillset of a law firm. It took three years of effort and investment before take-off really began.

Issues

The strategy we have followed since 2015 is to determine the cost of producing a Get Legal document as a bespoke document in the traditional way. We then price the Get Legal document at 10 percent of that cost, in the expectation that 10 sales online would make this approach successful. In reality, some automated documents sold vastly more, and some not at all. We have had to employ free and discounted offers, special cut priced bundles and free loss leaders, all to drive sales.

The biggest hurdle was to turn goodwill amongst lawyers towards Get Legal into automated documents that could be sold. In the end we produced an internal market whereby billing credit was received by the lawyer in the form of an advanced bill as soon as their document went live on the Get Legal website. That proved effective in getting sufficient documents for the Get Legal launch, but caused us problems in the nature of the document produced.

As soon as we launched the Get Legal service we realized that the marketplace was buying some documents but not others, and sales were generally disappointing. We had to feed this information back to our lawyers so that they did not produce documents that the marketplace would not buy.

We quickly found that we had opened a new BWB online "shop" selling initially automated document products, but in mid-2018, other fixed priced and added value services. Those added services include a fixed price, paid up front, review by a solicitor of the customer's Get Legal document, to ensure it was completely bespoke to the needs of that client.

Our major aim is to generate large volumes of website traffic and purchases, not specific financial targets at this stage. We want Get Legal to be the essential source of legal and other services for the smaller charity sector (which has several hundred thousand charities within it).

We will no longer internally fund Get Legal documents in areas that have proved unpopular with customers.

Data protection – a breakthrough

Whilst we were finding it very hard work to generate sales on documents which, looking back, we now realize were never going to be in high demand, the world beat a path to our Get Legal door to buy our data protection policy – compliant with the May 2018 GDPR Regulations.

Our initial priority had been business development to drive traffic to the Get Legal website – that is necessary but will fail on its own. We increasingly realized that if the user experience – particularly purchasing – on the website was not simple and the documents were not appealing and useful to customers, then we would fail.

Our new strategy is topical Get Legal documents produced at the time of maximum demand – not four months later. BD social media activity, a great user experience on the website with easy purchasing, and really attractive Get Legal documents produced on time, have proved to be the key to success.

As the new website enters ever more complex areas of service provision, the regulatory issues it needs to address become more complex. We are moving the client from automated document production to legal advice and then back to more document purchasing. This is clearly new territory, with some elements being within the definition of regulated activities for anti-money laundering. Those challenges are being addressed.

The future of law

Sales and non-sale income have been sufficiently robust to justify a new website being launched in May 2018. The new website will allow a fixed-price purchase of legal advice from a lawyer who can review and adapt the automated document to the very precise needs of the customer. This combination of low-cost automated legal document production, combined with focused face-to-face lawyer paid time, was Professor Richard Susskind's (the guru of AI in law) prediction of the future of law – 10 years ago.

We have begun to use Get Legal documents (with their low-cost of production) as the starting point for lawyers, using them as productivity tools upon which further bespoke work occurs, for the provision of traditional services to traditional clients.

We are planning to use expertise we have developed in automated document production to take our own specialist precedents and place them within the Q&A automated document format.

The online shop we have created – with large footfalls – is going to be used to sell other fixed price services, even though those services may be produced in the traditional way by lawyers. Many consumers – particularly millennials – are used to purchasing online. They will be fearful of the lawyers who charge by the hour, uncertain costs, cost overruns, and uncertain delivery timescales. For relatively narrow services, fixed price, paid for by credit card, over a fixed delivery time, will be the only way they will want to buy legal services.

In five years, Get Legal may have 500 Q&A automated legal documents on sale and a myriad of other services which are purchased like products.

In all of these cases we had not anticipated these opportunities opening up to us when we launched Get Legal in 2015. It is not been an easy road, but as these opportunities emerge, it places BWB in a very strong position to exploit the efficiencies and cost savings which this "AI Light" technology provides.

The legal market place for document automation

The majority of the marketplace is concentrating upon document production as a lawyer productivity tool, not as a client-facing service. We can fully understand why that should be the case from our experience with Get Legal. Almost 50 percent of the work we are undertaking on Get Legal is providing the context, advice, and hints for clients when completing their Get Legal Q&A.

The drive for automated Q&A seems to be led by Top 100 law firms using commercial products from the major legal technology precedent companies – PLC/Thomson Reuters and Lexis Nexis PSL plus Sysero.

Whilst there are some consumer-focused document production websites, there is no serious player aiming at corporate entities. Occasionally in some specialist sectors we find websites that give the impression of bespoke document production. However, on investigation, they are either selling flat precedents with minor mail merge of names and addresses, or the website is actually being used to sell traditionally delivered legal services. Some of those look attractive as a sales vehicle for traditional services.

The most comprehensive offering to date is probably the 300 current PLC precedents that Thompson Reuters have put into a document automated, Q&A format. Some of these are very complex precedents, requiring over 100 questions.

Initially, the impression was given that new software would be required to use this new format and like many other of their products, this new software would only be priced upon the total number of fee earners within the firm. For BWB's 100 lawyers, a figure of £200k is in my memory.

However, over a three-year period, that position has fundamentally changed, with PLC Q&A precedents being offered to current PLC subscribers at no additional cost. It is only if a firm wishes to use the automation software to produce its own bespoke automated documents, that paid licenses are required. Even then, the number of licences are based purely on the number of PCs that will be using the software to generate new bespoke Q&A precedents. Those licences are modestly priced per PC. Lexis Nexis has followed the same path. Sysero has good and competitively priced Q&A and workflow software for bespoke projects.

The reason for this surprising change on pricing is most likely that the software required to manage Q&A document automation is now not complex or expensive and the legal software suppliers cannot attempt to charge significant amounts for it.

In February 2018, Deloitte – which already provides legal services in many countries worldwide – announced it was applying for an ABS licence in the UK. Matt Ellis, managing partner for tax and legal, said:

"We do not want to replicate a traditional law firm. We're planning to use our technology and advisory skills to transform legal services."

How?

"By automating repetitive processes and completing routine tasks in a fraction of the time…"

Starting with a blank sheet and a focused strategy, with the advantage of the accountants' instinctive approach to process-driven service delivery and without all of the negative baggage of lawyers' reluctance to the perceived de-skilling of legal document automation, Deloitte will no doubt be a major disruptor of the current legal sector. Deloitte has the investment and management assets of a worldwide organization, and is bringing those resources to bear on the low hanging fruit of the current inefficient legal market. They will most likely take major market share. In this case their target client will be General Counsel of mid to large corporates – broadly the current client base of the legal Top 100.

Whilst it will benefit the mid-sized firm that Q&A automated precedents are being offered for free to current subscribers of PLC and Lexis

Nexis PSL, those are expensive base services. Firms that cannot afford the base precedent services will be squeezed even further as automation drives down the price of legal document production.

Case maps

Many firms have used workflow to manage cases for many years and software exists to help plan, construct, and manage legal workflow. The latest development is for the Q&A precedent suppliers to add on free case maps for a specific transaction. So, rather than the partner providing the guidance on the next step in this transaction after this document has been agreed, the map has already told you and offered you the next (possibly Q&A) precedent to best manage the next step. Those road maps could contain speed and cost indicators for a standard process. They could even anticipate the other side's likely negotiating strategy and suggest where you can concede and where you must hold firm. If a computer can beat the world chess champion by sheer brute processing power, it will soon manage a discrete adversarial legal negotiation.

Think of a case map as an automated case management system – potentially very powerful when combined with 100 percent Q&A documents within that process. When the software has access to hundreds or thousands of similar transactions and the outcome of different negotiating tactics, it can pick the best approach for this matter transaction and adapt as new information unfolds.

If the only constraint for the computer is sheer complexity and number of possible variants within a fixed set of rules, now there are no constraints. The processing power is now cheaply available to break through previous complexity constraints – and they will call it AI (and it is on my definition) – but the machine is not learning for itself. It is combining a human's programming skill with infinite processing power.

Impact on the current legal sector of legal document automation

In summary, if you are a small firm without access to purchasing the major precedent services, you are going to be priced out of many areas by the cost reductions achieved by document automation. Your savior might be to access low cost automation tools to gain your own advantage in narrow service lines.

If you are a mid-sized firm, you might find that your current protection from larger rivals – your lower cost and charge rates – will be eroded by

Top 100 firms investing heavily in automation and reducing their prices whilst maintaining their profitability (probably with some offshoring).

For the Top 100, be prepared for Deloitte to be coming after your General Counsel clients with offerings that are simply in a different league in terms of speed, price, and approach.

Reference

1. https://getlegal.bwbllp.com/

Chapter 6:
Democratizing the law by utilizing AI to reduce costs

By Andrew Arruda, CEO and co-founder, ROSS Intelligence

Much has been written about big law firms and their business models, and not much of it has been optimistic. With globalization, automation, and pure common sense, clients today expect more for their money. They are increasingly ordering basic legal services online, like wills and leases, and the average client is unable to spend $1,000 an hour for legal advice.

These days, there is a demand for more reasonable prices for services and not only in law. ROSS Intelligence builds artificially intelligent tools to enhance lawyers' abilities – allowing them to do more than ever before humanly possible.

As ROSS CEO and co-founder, I believe that everything has changed in the last ten years. Clients are now in control and want efficient legal service from their firms. We are in for some exciting times as legal technology continues to become an essential element of legal operations. The company's mission statement is:

"When we see the future, we envision a world where everyone has access to affordable legal representation."

This democratization of legal services will be where AI has its greatest impact.

The growing availability and practicality of artificial intelligence technologies such as machine learning and natural language processing within the legal sector has created a new class of tools that assist legal analysis within activities like legal research, discovery and document review, and contract review. Often, the promised value of these tools is significant, while lingering cultural reluctance and skepticism within the legal profession can lead to hyperbolic reactions to so-called "robot lawyers," both positive and negative. What is often lacking is evidence-based assessments of the impact of the growing market of AI-enabled legal tools on both the successful practice and business operations of legal organizations.

The ROSS Intelligence tool is an artificial intelligence platform supporting legal research activities. Built on ROSS Intelligence's proprietary legal AI framework, Legal Cortex, combined with technologies such as IBM Watson's cognitive computing technology, ROSS uses natural language processing and machine learning capabilities to identify legal authorities relevant to particular questions.

Users conduct searches by entering questions in plain language, rather than by complex search strings. ROSS's cognitive computing and semantic analysis capabilities permit the tool to understand the intent of the question asked and identify answers "in context" within the searched authorities.

The platform acts as a case law research supplement to traditional approaches used by electronic legal research tools. It provides increased research output quality (by collecting the most relevant authorities among its initial returned results) as well as a resulting improvement in the efficient execution of legal research activities when compared to the use of traditional tools alone.

We believe that by implementing technology in law practices, firms can become more profitable and efficient. And we believe in providing hard numbers to support this business case. Firms using ROSS have reported a 30 percent reduction in research time, and found 40 percent more relevant authorities, translating to an ROI of between 177 percent and 545 percent compared to core search alone.

In 2017, ROSS commissioned Blue Hill Group to assess the impact of ROSS-assisted use cases in bankruptcy law research with respect to:

- Information retrieval quality;
- Usability and user confidence; and
- Research efficiency.

Blue Hill used a panel of 16 legal researchers to benchmark primary ROSS use cases with those involving Boolean and natural language search capabilities of research platforms. It found that the ROSS tool provides significant, additive contributions to the effectiveness of legal researchers. These gains included a 22.3 percent to 30.3 percent reduction in research time, stemming from substantial improvements in information retrieval, particularly in the ranking of research results identified by a .61 NDCG score. These results have the potential to unlock new gains in the efficient and profitable operation of legal organizations, as well as create opportunities for new revenue gain.

Considering that industry calculations show a typical associate works an average of 743.6 hours a year completing legal research, and 26 percent of legal research time is written off as unbilled or unpaid by clients, this represents serious savings.

The following case study shows how this has been put into practice.

Van Horn Law Group

Van Horn Law Group is a Fort Lauderdale-based law firm comprised of three attorneys who practice and advise on a variety of personal and corporate bankruptcy matters. It handles the most Chapter 11 cases in the southern district of Florida. Through a combination of dedicated philanthropy, spirited entrepreneurship and legal expertise, managing partner Chad T. Van Horn applies his resources and networking to helping people and has emerged as a South Florida business leader. He says:

"We take a different approach to working with clients and to helping them reach their goals that we believe makes us capable of successfully guiding our clients."

After receiving several prestigious awards in 2016-17, growth in client demand was outpacing the firm's capacity to take on new work. Chad needed to find a solution that would buy his firm back more hours in the day while ensuring the high quality of service that their clients had come to expect.

"That's what sets us apart from the bigger law firm model, we can't bill millions of dollars in administrative fees. We don't have the capacity."

Looking for a tool to support its growing caseload and better serve its clients, the company adopted ROSS Intelligence, enabling it to cut down on difficult-to-bill research hours, allowing the firm to dedicate extra time towards working directly with its growing clientele.

"Part of the problem within the legal industry, is that it is built on inefficiencies," says Chad. "As for legal research, it is a challenge to know, when do I stop researching? It's hard to know if more hours will incre-men¬tally improve the quality of work.

"I want to save my clients admin¬istrative costs associated with their bankruptcy so they can put that money back into their company. I can only do this successfully by staying lean."

Getting the necessary work done for their clients while aiming to limit these overhead costs was proving more and more difficult. The Van Horn Law Group's existing legacy research tools were too time consuming, and increasingly difficult to navigate.

As a self-professed early adopter of new technologies, Chad recognized the need to stay ahead of the curve. When he first heard of ROSS Intelligence, he immediately understood the benefits ROSS could bring to the legal research process.

By adopting ROSS into his team for bankruptcy litigation support, Chad was quickly brought up to speed on new issues of law.

"ROSS provides a new, necessary baseline, which every lawyer will ulti¬mately come to rely on. As opposed to saying, 'we've been doing it this way for 10 years…' to persuade the local Bankruptcy judges, I now know I have the law on my side."

With only two Bankruptcy judges in the county where Van Horn Law Group is located, Chad recognizes that his professional reputation matters, and presenting favorable arguments grounded in the law should win the day. In addition, appeals are time consuming and expensive for clients, so getting things right the first time is paramount.

With a flat fee subscription, ROSS doesn't charge per use, meaning that Chad and his team can use it freely. "As a lawyer, I just want relevance", he says. "It's the Google mentality; with respect to research, I want to type into one place and get relevant results. And I think ROSS is better at getting me closer, faster."

ROSS Intelligence is now incorporated into the daily workflow at Van Horn Law Group, saving the firm countless hours on legal research while generating quality work product in bankruptcy law for the attorneys to rely on.

As a firm doing a significant amount of flat fee work, finding a tool that helps increase certainty while reducing research time is critical.

Says Chad:

"ROSS definitely saves my own time because we're a small firm. Where it saves me on research time it lets me concentrate more on getting the facts together with regards to a case and more on the customer service aspects, getting more time to speak with, prep and work with my clients. As well as giving me more confi¬dence in my argument, not only have I researched an issue but with AI behind me it gives me added legitimacy (as opposed to relying on a law clerk or associate to research it for me). I just have to apply the facts to the law at that point."

As a further testament to the Van Horn Law Group's exemplary service, Chad Van Horn was voted Pro Bono attorney of 2016 for Legal Aid in Broward County as well as 2017 Florida Big Brother of the Year by Big Brothers Big Sisters. He attributes his ability to focus his services on underrepresented community members in part on his adoption of ROSS.

"The time I saved using ROSS on research and writing has allowed me to dedicate more time into the pro bono space and provide better service."

Considering the highly documented unmet need for legal aid due to limited resources among those who need it, ROSS is helping lawyers like Chad get more time back in their day to better utilize their services, furthering ROSS' mission to democratize the law.

With respect to how other lawyers should incorporate ROSS into their practice, Chad says:

"I would recommend it to other lawyers as this is going to be the baseline moving forward. If lawyers aren't utilizing technology like this their client will suffer."

Conclusion

We are currently at an early stage in both the development and adoption of AI-assisted legal research and other legal tools. As the sophistication of these tools grows and use expands from early adopters to the wider legal community, the cycles of hype and anxiety that have colored the initial discourse surrounding AI tools will begin to give way to demand for evaluations of the tangible impact and value available through these tools.

While often in danger of overstatement, the impact of this AI-led stage of evolution is substantial. The improved accessibility of legal data, authorities, and commentary has eroded the traditional value proposition of the online research database – the aggregation and interrogation of large sets of legal sources. The emergence of low-cost and no-cost alternatives puts pressure on the pricing models of traditional tools, while simultaneously driving the need for differentiation through new functionality and features that provide enhanced utility, either by increasing the speed and effectiveness of research, or by unlocking new value from legal data.

With respect to the former, AI-assisted tools represent an improvement, by improving the interrogability of large sets of legal sources, while removing the labor-intensive manual indexing, classification, and passage identification traditionally used by legal publishers. Blue Hill's benchmark research reveals a concurrent improvement in effectiveness and efficiency compared to established approaches to legal research. In this way, AI-assisted tools such as ROSS Intelligence represent a clear response to the present market needs, delivering value through both cost of ownership and contributed value vectors. It is this combination that permits these tools to demonstrate net business gains and ROI in use cases that enhance, rather than replace, traditional research strategies.

Chapter 7:
iManage RAVN and Keoghs – streamlining the process of handling insurance disputes

By Dene Rowe, partner and director of product development, Keoghs

The insurance industry is currently going through radical change, adopting new technologies. As the introduction to a recent White Paper[1] on the subject puts it:

> *"Insurers are struggling to achieve profitable growth. There is constant pressure to launch new products and be responsive to the market as it develops; there is additional pressure to drive efficiency and reduce costs, without sacrificing quality. There's a renewed emphasis to improve the nature of the relationship with the client and agent, including supporting both across multiple channels seamlessly with a consistent experience. With the rise of the "internet of things" driving a fundamental shift in how insureds research and interact with businesses and individuals, insurers know they need to transform – not just to keep pace with technology, but to leverage it as a real competitive differentiator."*

Keoghs is quite unique in the legal industry in that it only serves the insurance markets. All our efforts and our endeavors are serving insurance companies, primarily in personal injury disputes. In total we have around 1,700 people spread throughout the UK. We've seen significant growth over the last two years, to the point where our annual revenues are now close to £100 million in turnover. In total, we handle around 100,000 claims per annum. As you can imagine, there is a large amount of process involved, so from our perspective we are an ideal candidate firm for automation and technology because of the sheer volume of transactions that we do in the legal sense.

Fundamentally, therefore, the first part of our AI initiative was to understand that, in order to continue to be relevant in this industry, we have to invest in the same areas as they are. There is quite a bit of pressure within the industry that we serve to implement this sort of technology.

Keoghs' AI initiative is focused on delivering innovative products to streamline the process of handling insurance disputes. In the first instance, what we did was look at the end-to-end process of how we actually carry out certain aspects of our work. We handle a large volume of low value personal injury disputes. What we wanted to do was look at our process management systems and in effect, layer artificial intelligence over the top of that, to automate the end-to-end process.

So instead of having lots of people handling these claims on behalf of the insurance company, the idea was to create a self-service initiative to allow the insurance company to do it themselves. Fundamentally, what we wanted to do with AI was bring different services to the insurance market, and on that basis, that was the opportunity that sparked our interest.

The first thing we brought to market was what we call the avoidable litigation product. We identified that this was ripe for this kind of automation because it could be given to the insurance company to settle the claim, without us having any human involvement.

iManage RAVN

iManage RAVN is a leading provider of work product management solutions for law firms, corporate legal departments, and other professional services firms such as accounting and financial services. iManage Extract, which is the product we are using, uses AI technology to automatically read, extract, and interpret critical business information from large volumes of documents and unstructured data. With iManage Extract, we're able to gain greater efficiencies by integrating the solution within our own AI platform, specifically focusing on the automation of document extraction and review, allowing for a more productive environment.

We chose iManage RAVN because, during the proof of concept phase, it was able to perform very successfully the two main things we needed – which was to extract unstructured data and turn it into structured data, and then to provide contextual data, to allow us to base decisions on that data.

Millions of labor hours are spent every year by smart (and expensive) law firm associates rifling through agreements and extracting key data that is used in crucial transactional documents and analysis. This manual, labor-intensive effort is very expensive, time consuming, prone to errors, and impacts overall company competitiveness. This labor cost can eat away at profitability or even make entire practices of business too expensive to pursue.

Many organizations faced with this challenge are exploring the use of AI technology to streamline their business processes. AI's ability to quickly automate cognitive tasks enables firms to dramatically reduce or eliminate the time consuming and costly work of reviewing and extracting key terms from thousands of disparate documents.

In simple terms, what the iManage tool allows us to do is take the unstructured documents we receive – so for example, the client forms, medical reports and so on – and dive into that information and extract data (such as the claimant name, defendant name, the date of medical examination etc.) and turn that into structured data.

We can also use the tool to read the document and put some context around it, so that we can make decisions on them. For instance, the program will go into the medical report, extracting and reading and interpreting what that medical report is saying, in effect mimicking what a lawyer would do with that report. So, we're teaching the computer ultimately to read what's in front of them.

The important thing for us was adding an API into that world, because we wanted to automate the end-to-end process. It was no good just creating a separate process where people were reviewing the outputs. The API that we were able to create with iManage and RAVN means that within our end-to-end process we are able to return the results back to the AI engine, which allows us to make further automations into our process management system. It is really a principal part of the end-to-end process.

iManage Extract

iManage Extract automatically reads, extracts, and interprets critical business information from large volumes of documents and unstructured data, all from a single user interface. With iManage Extract, organizations can typically reduce manual labor costs by 50 percent or more, and transform unmanageable projects into streamlined and profitable processes.

iManage Extract quickly identifies the structure of a document and uses out-of-the box or self-trained extractors to accurately find and extract specific terms or clauses.

We started developing our own AI platform earlier this year, but a key missing component was how we would look to extract data from unstructured data sources efficiently. iManage Extract complements and perfectly integrates with our AI platform to help create a suite of unique products in the marketplace where significant portions of the litigation process are not processed by humans. We see this as a clear competitive advantage in what is a dynamic market.

We carried out the proof of concept just over 12 months ago, and we started to develop products and services on the back of that. It's really only in the last six months that we've been using it in the wild, so to speak.

It was an executive-level board decision to start the process. I took the lead role of pushing this forward, and we ring fenced the investment for this using executive board level sponsorship.

Better than a human

In the main, because it's focused on the client, the lawyers like it, because it gives them an additional USP. With their sales head on they can go and work with the clients and say look how innovative we are, doing this type of work. It demonstrates that they are ahead of the competition, which is very useful for anyone in a client-facing role. Obviously, whenever you introduce new technology there can be resistance. There is this perception of robots taking over the world! But fundamentally it has been very easy to work with, because the lawyers have helped design and develop it. They've got to be in at the heart of this because, ultimately, it's their knowledge we're leveraging. It gives us an extra USP, and is a real differentiator for the competitive market that we're in.

If you understand that smart AI technology is not here to replace human lawyers but to make you a better lawyer that forces you to use your instinct, emotional intelligence, and capitalize on your mind, then you have made the first step in future-proofing your business. iManage engineers and architects, along with other AI innovators, have spent years studying the technology, painstakingly developing, building and managing the smartest robotic systems. For machines to learn, they must be fed massive sets of data. And it is humans, with all our inherent faults and genius, who are doing the feeding.

From the lawyers' perspective, the change management process has been negligible. We're very lucky with the Keoghs culture, in that we're quite forward-thinking. We've been using automation in our case management system and workflow systems for the last 15 years, so we were already halfway along this journey anyway in terms of understanding. So, it's only been an incremental shift.

It has also improved over time. When we started off, looking for data points within the unstructured documents, we might only be getting 65 or 70 percent accuracy. Some people might consider that pretty poor, but if you consider your barometer should be human performance, you're never going to reach 100 percent anyway.

In my experience a human might get it right nine times out of 10, so your barometer should actually be to get the computer to get it right nine times out of 10, rather than 100 percent. And it's now performing at around 80 percent, but with the added bonus that it's doing it in a fraction of the time. So, if the benchmark is getting it to be better than a human, we're comfortable with how it's performing.

The future

I think there will come a point at which we say we're not going to invest in a particular technology any further than it needs to go, because it's at its optimum. I think if you can automate where you get to a solution where it's at 80 percent, then that's good enough.

I can see that by 2020, or 2021, about 60 to 70 percent of this high volume, low value, work will be automated. It's taken us about 18 months to go from vision to delivery, so we're looking at very short timescales for further development.

If you look at the legal services world, there are certain parts of the process – like reviewing contracts and carrying out due diligence – that are unavoidably going to use AI in the future. I do not see how a law firm in the future can hope to be around and relevant in the future without making an investment in AI.

Reference:
1. *Artificial intelligence in insurance*, Pega Insurance, 2017

Chapter 8:
How technology and AI is changing the legal value chain

By Karl Chapman, CEO, Riverview Law

In their book, *Remaking Law Firms*,[1] Dr. Imme Kaschner and Dr. George Beaton observe:

> *"Based on the researched conclusion that no law firm can assume its place and prosperity are assured… most firms are not well equipped to know what to do or how to 'remake' their business models. In the future the ways clients meet their needs and the rules for success of firms are very different. The winners in the kaleidoscope will be those firms that are starting now to prepare in earnest."*

They suggest that over the next decade there will be a series of trends that inevitably result in a reduction in the share of legal services revenues secured by traditional law firms. They forecast that, while still important, law firms will be substituted with a combination of new entrants, automation, technology innovation, and the continuing growth in corporate legal functions doing work that previously went externally. The figures below illustrate the Kaschner/Beaton forecast for the US and Western Europe. They identify the same trend in other jurisdictions. We witness these themes in all our customers.

There are lots of drivers behind this shift; increased speed of competition across all sectors, cost pressures, digital disruption, technological innovation including AI, law firm inertia… Significantly, we should not confuse the growth in work being retained by corporate legal functions with an inevitable growth in legal team numbers. Self-service, functions deciding (rightly) not to do certain things, and the adoption of technology will drive significant productivity gains. Corporations' enterprise-wide focus on data, from which legal operations is not immune, will accelerate this trend.

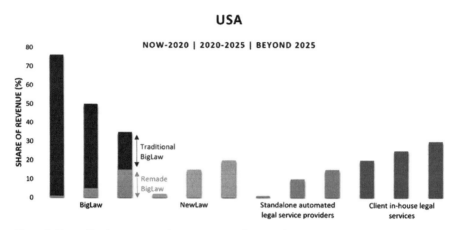

Figure 1: Types of legal service provider in US, now and projected

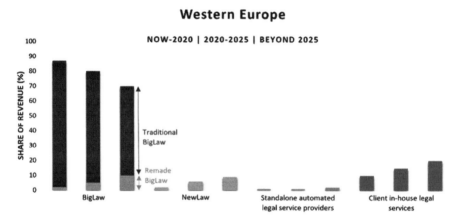

Figure 2: Types of legal service provider in Western Europe, now and projected

Riverview Law's AI journey

"I wouldn't start from here…"

We're often struck, inevitably unfairly on occasions, by a similar thought when we either read about the current and potential use of Artificial Intelligence (AI) in the legal market or discuss developments with potential customers or solutions providers.

Putting to one side the challenge that AI means many different things to many different people, I should state right up front that we are believers. We have absolutely no doubt that AI and related technology trends will have a significant impact on all markets and value chains. The legal market, globally, is not immune from this.

As a result, the Riverview Law Board has placed its bets and organized Riverview Law accordingly. We invested millions of pounds in "Kim", a New Jersey-based knowledge automation and workflow platform.

Kim is a virtual assistant to knowledge workers in all sectors. Through its no-code configuration model, Kim enables knowledge workers, including lawyers, to take control of their critical business processes and work to make better and quicker decisions. Kim does this by utilizing its patent pending artificial intelligence, assimilation and, critically, data management capabilities. We believe that the direction of travel is clear, even if timing is unpredictable, and have acted accordingly.

It is from this position of belief that we have what is hopefully a helpful reflection. From much of the activity that we see in the legal market we suspect that, with exceptions, many organizations are starting their AI journey from the wrong place (the outside in). We sense that much energy, money, and time is being (and will be) wasted chasing fash-ion-driven AI point solutions rather than proper investment, problem solving, and experimentation using platforms. Indeed, much of the effort we see in this area can be put in the "being seen to be doing something" box. At the end of such a process the inevitable happens. Expectations are disappointed. The technology is blamed. Future investments are delayed or shelved.

This chain of events is potentially life-threatening to organizations. Failure to understand and ride the current data, IT, and AI wave, over time, risks all. It is a bet the firm issues … particularly if the wrong or no bets are placed!

Given the technological and data revolution we are living through, inaction is highly dangerous. But the irony in legal is that the risks can be reduced, and the opportunities of success increased, by learning from other industries, and in particular from house builders.

Lessons learnt – from house builders!

Typically, you would not build a house from the roof down. But that is what we see happening in many law firms and organizations, with some notable exceptions (Vodafone, Barclays, HSBC, Allen & Overy, DWF, Pinsent, some of the Big Four). There is a temptation to seek instant solutions. Under pressure to respond to noise and market trends, companies appear to be trying to put the AI roof on the house without building or re-constructing the foundations, walls and floors first. As Professor Stephen Mayson observed when I discussed this with him:

"They aren't even building the roof. Many have just bought some tiles and are now trying to work out what to do with them."

By the way, we recognize this process because this is exactly what we tried to do when we started our AI journey in 2013. We made many mistakes and learnt many interesting lessons. Which is why the house building analogy resonates so strongly with us now.

If you have ever watched a house being built from scratch, two things will probably have struck you. Firstly, a long time seems to pass with very little progress being made, even though there is a full building crew on-site. Then, suddenly, when the foundations are finished, the house takes shape remarkably quickly. One morning the site is just concrete foundations and ground works, and the next day the house starts to emerge, proudly, from its rock-solid foundations. It is almost as if it is saying, "I was always here but you couldn't see me".

Secondly, in those weeks when you saw little progress being made, you were probably also surprised by how small the building footprint was. Clearly, a relatively small house is being built on the plot. But, when the house starts going up, you are amazed by how big it actually is, given how small the foundations and footprint appeared.

This is where the fundamental role played by the foundations comes into play. In the house that has been built there are many different rooms; lounge, dining room, kitchen, bedrooms, bathroom… The four bedrooms are all different; in shape, decoration and furniture. But, critically, all the rooms, with their different functions and designs, are built on the same foundations.

The picks and shovels of the digital, disruptive, and AI age (it is all about the data)

Mark Twain famously observed that "during the gold rush it's a good time to be in the pick and shovel business".

The picks and shovels of this digital, disruptive, and AI age are data, context, and no-code configurable software tools. If legal embraces these picks and shovels and pursues a function-wide data strategy, it will find itself at the center of organizational decision-making.

Imagine:

- Quantitative legal and related workflow and process data that provides a foundational data and integration layer;
- Qualitative data that builds context from the inside out and which enables AI; and
- Legal data that, when coupled with no-code configurable software tools and platforms such as Kim, results in subject and domain experts, with no IT development expertise at all, creating, evolving, and distributing legal tools and solutions both internally within an organization, and/or more widely to a supply chain or the market generally.

All within hours and days rather than weeks and months.

In a legal context, imagine if:

- All the 90 percent+ of non-sensitive instructions coming into a corporate legal department (or law firm!) that cannot be self-served or that should be re-directed, are complete, actionable and routed automatically to the appropriate individual, team, or third party to handle. Our data shows that typically more than 70 percent of the instructions coming into corporate legal departments are incomplete, generating significant failure demand, frustration and lots of "noise".[2]
- The first time a lawyer sees a customer or supplier contract that needs legal input is version three. Version one was both automatically generated when procurement or sales completed a legal request and then sent it to the counter-party. If the counter-party marks up the contract rather than e-signing it, it becomes version two and is routed to the appropriate team/lawyer, internally or externally depending on the document type, risk, and any other criteria. The lawyer/team member now works on version three.[3]
- A general counsel (or managing partner) can see all the live cases/ matters being handled by the function (law firm), whether they are being handled internally or externally. What their status, risk, and value is. Who is handling the work. What the value of all procurement/sales contracts are overall and by sales product, procurement category, geography, supplier/customer. What litigation exposure there is and what the sources of the issues are.

> What leases are in renewal, etc. That s/he can also see the trend data for all activity, which enables the evolution of the function-wide operating model.[4]

This is the world we live in now. It all starts with the critical legal operations data layer and a function-wide strategy.

The need for legal operating platforms

Legal market culture, which is molded by tradition and law firm models that reward hourly billing, hardly encourages or embeds a general understanding of the value that technology and data can bring to decision-making, customer service, process improvement, and operating models. Lawyers tend not to understand data, data layers, data integrity, or operating models – but operations does!

Tellingly, we have seen a significant divergence in the last few years between law firms and corporate legal departments (a trend that coincides with the rise of legal operations and CLOC). With some notable exceptions, law firms are slow adopters of models and tools that capture data and help them tell actionable stories that increase quality, speed up decision-making, manage risk, and reduce costs. At the same time, in-house legal departments are embracing data and technology opportunities with the zeal of the convert *precisely because* it increases quality, speeds decision-making, manages risk, and reduces costs! It enables them to do more with less at a time when budgets are under pressure and demands on their services are increasing.

Put simply, corporate legal departments have the drivers for change. Their organizations are under intense margin and competitive pressures, while law firms, many of whom are still making excess profits, do not. Their organizations are demanding quicker response times and data-driven decisions.

This thirst for data by in-house legal teams, and the consequential adoption of technology, is and will have a significant impact on department legal operating models, law firms, and the structure of the supply chain. This inevitability is highlighted by a simple example. "Triage" is one of the most powerful words in the corporate legal dictionary. It is the foundational layer that drives not only a game-changing data strategy but the entire legal operating model. Triage makes sure that the right work is undertaken by the right people, at the right time, and at the right price, whether that work is done internally or externally.

Because triage captures the data automatically, we see our corporate customers start, quickly, to re-allocate work. It is amazing how often the data highlights experienced in-house team members working on matters that are mid- or low-complexity, while work they can, should, and want to do is being sent to expensive external law firms. By allocating the work properly, in-house morale increases because the team is working on more challenging matters. Net costs reduce because expensive, hourly-billing, third-party law firms are replaced by a combination of self-service, in-house team members and/or fixed-priced, managed services providers handling the volume day-to-day work. The data allows corporate legal functions to answer what, in reality, are pretty fundamental questions; how many matters do we have live today, where did they come from, what is their risk profile, who is handling them, what is their status?

In this context, legal is no different from any other function in a business. If you ask a finance director equivalent questions – what is our net cash position, what is the rolling three-month cash-flow and how does it compare with budget, how is our capital expenditure tracking against forecast? – they can answer immediately. If you ask a sales director what the sales pipeline looks like, they can comment on the number of opportunities in the pipeline, by product, country, business unit, who is handing them, what the status by opportunity is, and their forecast for the next week, month, and three months.

Legal does not have an operations platform. Finance, HR, and sales all have a range of platforms to select from – such as SAP, Oracle, Sage, Workday, and Salesforce. Legal is not just a poor relation; it is actually in a worse position. It has a series of point solutions that do not talk to each other (matter management, e-billing, document review), that have different data layers, and do not enable AI on an enterprise level because there is no context. They have no overarching and comprehensive reporting solution. No platform. Little accurate data.

All roads lead to legal operations platforms, not point solutions. To the legal data layer, not spreadsheets! The legal functions (and law firms) that grasp this on a function-wide basis move, quietly and unassumingly, to the center of organizational decision making, and will become game changers.

References

1. www.remakinglawfirms.com/
2. The data layer includes instructor details, work types, business units, case

statuses, case close reasons – a function-wide process data layer that enables live and trend dashboards, search and integration with other systems.

3. All templates are uploaded into Kim (the technology used by Riverview Law). All headings (e.g. Termination Provisions, Assignment, etc.) are consistent. The organization's preferred positions (clauses) by heading and by template are contained in a living playbook creating that organization's context, the way it contracts. This drives self-service, document automation, and negotiation and the review of third party paper, all from one function-wide contract management data layer.

4. As reference 1 but with primary, secondary, tertiary, and quaternary work types, case statuses by work types, case close reasons by work type, etc.

Chapter 9:
The diverse world of legal AI use cases

By Richard Tromans, innovation consultant, TromansConsulting and editor, ArtificialLawyer.com

Introduction

Readers of this book will no doubt by now have read several real-world use cases of legal AI technology. The examples earlier in this publication will have set out what certain vendors can do and why those applications matter to law firms and their clients.

This chapter seeks to place these individual applications inside a broader, global, picture of what is happening now and what is possible with legal AI technology. That is to say, we are long past the days of talking about "what could be done" or "robot lawyers" and the like. Legal AI is here, it's real, and it's happening now, all around the world.

The diversity of legal AI applications

An appreciation of how versatile natural language processing (NLP), machine learning, and expert systems can be is central to what I term "the new wave of legal technology"; that is to say, legal tech that *performs work*, rather than just being a basic utility, such as a document management system, which stores legal data. When one appreciates what this tech can achieve in a world where most of a lawyer's work involves written text, then seeing its diverse use cases makes a lot more sense.

This machine-supported legal work is what we can term "cognitive labor", such as reading and comprehension of unstructured data, i.e. legal text, the provision of legal information in response to questions, or automated legal data analysis that can support predictions about litigation outcomes.

A key reason that NLP and machine learning applications are so diverse is because they reflect the reality of commercial law.

The legal world is a broad and multi-practice focused sector, ranging from M&A to patents to litigation, with much in between. Meanwhile, the needs of private practice lawyers and those in corporate legal functions also vary, though also overlap. Also, there are many stages in any legal process, from negotiation, to contract completion, to post-completion review, to disputes based on those completed contracts. In short, it's a complex environment of multiple steps and pathways.

Moreover, there are large numbers of people, such as sales teams inside banks and corporates, who also handle what are essentially legal contracts, even if they are not lawyers. Non-lawyers in companies may also be responsible for procurement contracts or sending out NDAs. So, the variety of people involved also expands, which further increases the potential use cases for legal AI tech.

These sales and procurement contracts, or NDAs, can, under NLP analysis, also reveal value and insight that may have been overlooked before, in part because the review of contracts, especially in large volumes, can be seen as "process work" that does not merit the time and cost of senior lawyers' minds and their deep consideration. Or the same technology is used for review of contracts that are still not complete, often helping non-lawyers to complete tasks without sending the matter to the in-house legal team.

All in all, this means that the stakeholders of the legal world are many, and their needs are complex and multiple. It is then perhaps only fitting that this new wave of legal technology – that performs legal work – is also now diverse.

Global diversity

Before looking at some examples of legal AI tech in more detail, let us briefly mention another aspect of legal AI's diversity, and that refers to the geographical spread of the technology.

Although there are several legal AI companies in the US and UK, Toronto in Canada has quickly become a key center for legal tech and legal AI, with companies such as Kira Systems and Diligen based there, with Beagle.ai, based not far outside.

Across Europe, Berlin and Paris have also become centers for legal AI companies, from Leverton in Germany to Predictice in Paris. More recently, we have seen the development of legal AI companies in India – at least four at last count. China is also focused on this area. One US company, Seal Software, also has an office in Egypt, the first legal AI company to operate in North Africa.[1]

Moreover, in terms of the actual use of these systems, it is also a global picture. As one might expect, the large transactional law firms based often in the US or UK have been major adopters of AI tech, but uptake is now quite global. Firms from Spain and the Nordics[2] to Singapore[3] and Australia have now adopted legal AI solutions.

Therefore, it is a truly diverse, global, and complex ecosystem of vendors, law firm users, and corporates, who are all part of a wider group of stakeholders. Let no one tell you legal AI is "just a flash in the pan", or some isolated event in one or two markets that will fade away soon. It is far too integrated now at a global level to do anything other than keep growing.

The multiple branches of legal AI
Document review – legal AIs

The exact data on user uptake is still a grey area, but it is clear that use of AI document review systems for matters such as due diligence are one of the most popular use cases.

At last count, there were over 17 legal AI companies working across this market segment alone, both among law firms and corporates. Some of the better-known systems – many of which are participants in this book – include Kira Systems, iManage/RAVN, Luminance, LawGeex, and Seal Software, but there are many more.

As readers who work as lawyers will know well, due diligence can be very much a "process" task, often delegated to junior lawyers and/or paralegals. Clients are increasingly cost-averse about this work and AI systems have a very clear application, e.g. if a client doesn't want to pay for the use of junior lawyers to spot anomalies in a stack of 10,000 contracts, this is exactly the type of work an AI system – once trained to a sufficient level of accuracy – can achieve.

AI document review systems are by no means a "magic bullet". But they are tremendously useful. Training takes unbillable time, and lawyers can see this as a barrier. But, once trained up for a task that will be repeated, e.g. checking for certain types of clause in a type of contract a practice group often has to review, then that training can be seen as a "sunk cost", which is quickly amortised.

One question that is often also raised is whether NLP review systems are accurate enough. Tests by law firms and corporates have shown that, despite some cynicism, document review systems can indeed meet or better human review levels of accuracy and recall. This has surprised some lawyers, who still feel a bit uncomfortable at the idea a trained piece of software is more accurate than they are at review of legal documents.

As to the law firms that have publicly said they are using legal AI systems for document review, the list would fill half this page, especially if we included every country where they are used. Suffice it to say here, legal AI document review is very real, and very present already in the market.

That in turn is changing client expectations, and we are also seeing LPOs and alternative legal service providers such as Axiom, Elevate, and Contract Pod, making use of NLP systems in the same way.

This area is probably the most widespread legal AI use case, at least beyond the natural language review systems used by e-discovery companies.

Risk, compliance, and playbooks

The same review technology can also be used in a more focused way to isolate issues that an in-house team may have with a contract.

That is to say, the system is trained to respond to the company's legal "playbook", which covers areas such as agreed compliance boundaries, acceptance of certain terms, and pre-set risk levels in the wording of a contract. Examples include ThoughtRiver and LegalSifter, both of which work with law firms and corporates.

The aim here is not to do reviews of thousands of contracts per day, but to create an automated method for fast review in a company, or a law firm in some cases, so that the lawyers can focus on other matters, or only focus on a contract when it is "flagged" by the system as problematic.

Some of these systems can also be designed to include "guide books" that help the lawyer conducting the review. Often the focus is on contracts that have yet to be signed off, as opposed to post-completion review.

Whatever the specific design, the overall aim is the same – to speed the review process through pre-trained automation and, where possible, to add extra value through providing automated input and risk spotting. This allows lawyers, whether in a firm or working in a company, to focus on more complex matters.

Predictive systems and research

The reality is that lawyers don't have to use machine learning and NLP to find useful data in a stack of previous dispute documents to predict what will happen with a similar case.

Lawyers could look at, for example, the last 100 liability claims they handled for an insurance company, examine key data points such as cost of claim, number that succeeded – and any related reasons why – as well as points such as length of time to process the claim and the total cost in lawyers' time. That will help the firm and the client to decide what claims to settle and which to focus on – and to do this based on past data, rather than a personal view.

However, using NLP allows a law firm or client to do much, much more. For example, rather than manually analysing 100 previous disputes to isolate patterns in a set of similar matters, they could examine hundreds, or even thousands of cases, if they had the available data and the time to train the system to extract meaningful data.

Whether law firms do this themselves, or work with legal tech vendors, there are huge opportunities to analyze past cases to help predict outcomes in current matters. The "AI aspect" is simply bringing a higher level of scale and likely faster processing of the matter in hand. However, this can be the difference between a law firm conducting such an analysis or not. After all, analyzing hundreds of past cases by hand – especially if this is unbillable time – is a major hurdle for most lawyers in private practice.

Areas where we have seen this are in examples such as RAVEL and Lex Machina, which are now both part of Lexis Nexis, and which cover US case law, right down to helping assess how certain judges may respond to the request for a particular motion.

We also have examples such as the UK-based CaseCrunch, which last year famously modelled the likely outcome of consumer claims against banks for mis-selling insurance products.[4] In that example, the company asked lawyers to also attempt to predict the outcome of sample claims, while the CaseCrunch system used the model it had developed from examining past cases. The result? The predictive system beat the human lawyers.

Meanwhile, IBM's US-based legal AI team, working with its Watson Knowledge Studio tech, is exploring the development of "reasoning" applications that provide useful indicators to how a certain case may turn out.[5] This is done by again analyzing previous examples to create a model that can respond to new cases.

However, insights into case law are not only for prediction. Systems such as ROSS Intelligence are providing lawyers with new approaches to legal research, by exploiting NLP and machine learning. We also have companies such as Casetext offering the ability to "drag and drop" a legal brief into its CARA system and which will then rapidly provide detailed information on related cases and legal issues.

Again, the benefit here is two-fold: first there is the efficiency gain, because this tech can operate far faster than a human could; and second there is *the added value of new insights* that in many cases would have been missed without the data-crunching and comprehension powers of AI systems.

In short, these applications don't replace lawyers, but they provide a service that most lawyers simply would not have the time or resources to achieve on their own, or at least do so well or thoroughly. That perhaps is where legal AI shows its greatest value – *it augments the human lawyer*, rather than replacing them.

And there is more…

What is outlined above is just a taster of a far bigger and more complex picture that cannot be squeezed into this short chapter. Other areas that we can briefly mention are behavior prediction systems that are used in the US to help with jury selection, which analyse a juror's public data and social media posts to decide if they are sympathetic to a trial lawyer's arguments.

Another is expert systems, perhaps what we can call the true ancestor of all legal AI applications, as it was here in trying to model human logic that AI systems began in the 1950s and 60s. Today we see several expert systems companies, such as Neota Logic (based in the US, but which operates globally), Rainbird (based in the UK), and Berkeley Bridge (based in the Netherlands), all providing platforms that allow a team of lawyers to crystallise their knowledge and create an automated Q&A system that can lead a client to a useful answer to a legal question.

And then we could look at how contracting automation tools, which are not specifically "AI applications" can tap the data collected by the contracting tools using NLP to provide legal and business intelligence to companies.

The list goes on. But there is one thing that unites them all – looking at legal documents and legal knowledge as something that can be framed and understood using digital tools. This is something new. So too is the work that the AI tools perform. As mentioned at the start, they are literally performing aspects of legal work; this is also new.

AI technology doesn't have to be there for a technical application to be very useful, but those applications that do have NLP and machine learning capabilities are indeed special and powerful – and most of all, when they begin to be used at scale across a law firm, then they truly have a strategic impact.

I would encourage all lawyers to consider how such technology can be of benefit to their firm or in-house legal team, and their internal and external clients.

References

1. www.artificiallawyer.com/2017/10/03/legal-ai-pioneer-seal-software-opens-in-egypt-in-global-first.
2. www.artificiallawyer.com/2017/12/11/nordics-embrace-legal-ai-as-luminance-bags-maqs.
3. www.artificiallawyer.com/2017/10/11/legal-ai-co-luminance-sees-singapore-growth-with-rajah-tann.
4. www.artificiallawyer.com/2017/10/28/ai-beats-human-lawyers-in-casecrunch-prediction-showdown.
5. www.artificiallawyer.com/2018/02/20/integra-to-crowdsource-legal-ai-applications-with-ibm-watson-tech.

Chapter 10:
Technology, convergence, and the transformation of legal services

By Robert Millard, director, Cambridge Strategy Group

Of itself, disruptive technology does not transform industries. Creating new business models, that link that new technology to client needs, transforms industries. Those client needs might already exist (legal needs in this case) or they might be needs that are triggered by the impact of that technology. We are currently seeing a plethora of new digital technologies, and this book contains case studies where law firms are using some of them to good effect. In almost all cases, firms are using these technologies to:

- React to a client need that has emerged as a result of the impact of emergent technologies on their own businesses; and/or

- Become more efficient or otherwise competitive, using their existing business model.

Most law firms are using a business model that emerged in the early to mid-20th century, as a result of the disruptive technological innovations of the late 19th century. Of course, law firms have become larger and far more sophisticated since then. The advent of the internet and the personal computer in the early 1990s provided tools that have made the practice of law far more efficient. It also reduced the entry barriers to clients developing their own in-house legal departments and new kinds of legal service providers. The essential core of the business model, however, remains the people-leveraged pyramid first described in 1992 by Marc Galanter and Thomas Palay at the University of Chicago, in their book, *Tournament of Lawyers: The Transformation of the Big Law Firm*. In that book, they demonstrated how the success of large law firms stems from their ability to blend the talents of experienced partners with those of energetic junior lawyers, who are driven by a powerful incentive – to win a place in the partnership.

The case studies in this book are early indicators of trends that in due course will cause a transition to one or more radically different business models. Value creation will be driven by leveraging digital technology as well as people, as primary units of production. This is a trend to be embraced, not only because it is inevitable but because the emerging digital disruptions are creating a new generation of legal needs that are too complex and diffuse to be dealt with by people alone. Lawyers unable to use these fundamentally more comprehensive digital tools will find themselves functionally unable to advise their clients. At least, not without being guilty of malpractice.

Changing business models is incredibly difficult in businesses that are not only trading but doing so in the hyper-competitive markets we have today. Also, nowhere are the barriers to change more challenging than where the business has previously thrived under its current business model. For the leaders of such businesses, the call for change is a message that is counter-intuitive and conflicts with personal experience of what leads to success. In this lies the existential challenge of our time – for law firm leaders to build compelling business cases for change, that their partners will not only accept but embrace, and to map out a route to navigate the firm through the obstacles involved.

In order to build a case for change where the need for that change is not universally accepted, and furthermore the way forward is not clear, it usually helps to start from the ground up. We can do that from two perspectives, which are to:

- Trace the origins of the current "Tournament of Lawyers" model and its roots in the disruptive technological innovations of the late 19th century; and

- Examine the concept of convergence, which shows how single change drivers do not create their most transformational in isolation of each other but rather as a result of their complex, dynamically interconnected, influences on each other and their environment.

This chapter will look at these in turn, and then conclude with what some law firms currently are doing, and what others could do, to rise to this challenge.

The roots of the current large law firm business model

A different law firm business model existed before the "Tournament of Lawyers" model. The transition to that model was as disruptive, in many ways, as the disruption that is occurring today. It was described by a lawyer, Julius Cohen, in a book entitled *The Law: Business or Profession?* published in 1916. Cohen was born in 1873 and died in 1950. Over his lifetime, he witnessed radically disruptive technological change, driven primarily by the invention of distributed electricity, the internal combustion engine, telephone, and radio. Over his lifetime, Cohen witnessed the transition from:

- candles for lighting to electric lightbulbs and electrical appliances;
- animal-drawn transport and steam railways to automobiles;
- sailing ships to aircraft carriers and submarines;
- Morse code telegraphy to television;
- helium and hot-air balloons to jet passenger aircraft and the first rocket launch from Cape Canaveral;
- slide rules to mainframe computers; and
- surgery without proper anesthetics to modern medicine.

It would be difficult to argue that the technological advances that western society has experienced over the past 50 years are anything like as transformational as these.

For the legal profession, the impact of these new technologies on western financial institutions, corporates, and governments were especially important. Over the course of Julius Cohen's lifetime, the legal needs of sophisticated western business clients were utterly transformed. Perhaps triggered at least in part by the invention of the offset lithographic paper printing press in 1906, the amount of legislation burgeoned. Driven by landmark legislation such as (in the United States) the Sherman Antitrust Act and the Glass-Steagall Act, so too the complexity involved in legal compliance. Two booms in M&A took place during this era. The first was in the final decade of the 19th century and involved more than 15 percent of the assets in the US market. The second commenced in 1910, accelerated after the end of World War I, and lasted until the onset of the Great Depression in 1929. These triggered the emergence of modern corporate law.

As the scale and complexity of business clients' legal needs grew, lawyers were forced to specialize. Where an individual lawyer had been adequate on a matter before, teams became necessary. Practice groups emerged. The billable hour was invented by Reginald Heber Smith, then managing partner of Boston firm Hale & Dorr (now part of WilmerHale.) Junior lawyers' time started to be billed to clients, and quickly this leverage became an important profit driver in the business model. By the 1970s, the largest firms in the world had several hundred lawyers and several had opened international offices.

The golden age of the "Tournament of Lawyers" model was probably from the 1960s to the 1980s. Apart from the occasional recession, strong economic growth and hence demand for legal services was sustained. Globalization commenced in earnest and another M&A boom emerged, this time from the mid-1950s until the mid-1970s, followed by a fourth wave from 1984 to 1989. In the absence of the digital tools that lawyers take for granted today, the only way to leverage was through people. The business model pyramid hierarchy of partners doing the most difficult, high value work and junior lawyers doing the simpler, less expensive work (and learning in the process) worked very well.

From the 1990s onwards, the advent of digital technologies started to exert pressure on the "Tournament of Lawyers" model. This era saw the transition of the architecture and engineering firms, amongst others, from people-leveraged business models with drawing boards and pens, to digitally-leveraged business models with people, heavily enabled by "computer aided design" (CAD). Regulatory protection and market demand through first the dotcom boom of the late 1990s then the credit boom of 2001-09 softened the impact on law firms, but the share of legal work done by conventional law firms with "Tournament of Lawyers" business models has been steadily decreasing since then. In-house legal departments and new kinds of legal service providers have been steadily capturing market share held previously by conventional law firms. The "Big Four" global advisory firms started to build their legal services again, along with other non-audit, advisory work. By the end of 2017, the Big Four accounted for roughly 40 percent of the world's $155bn management consultancy spend. They collectively employed close to 10,000 lawyers and had started to appear in league tables such as Legal 500 and Chambers and partners. It makes no sense, as some law firms do, to continue to refer to them (frequently pejoratively) as "accounting firms" (see Figure 1).

As this is being written in 2018, law firms are experiencing a modest uptick again in demand. This is driven by client activity fueled by cheap credit and other facets of the continued regulatory response to the global financial crisis of 2008/09. Some law firms appear to be taking this respite as evidence that business model transformation may not be necessary.

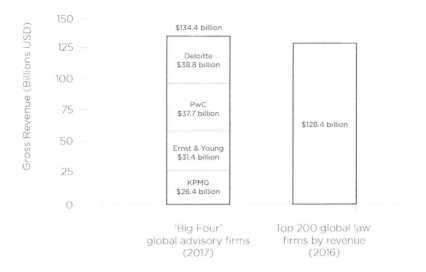

Figure 1: The revenues of the Big Four global advisory firms in 2017 were almost the same as the 200 largest law firms in the world by revenue, in 2016. (Sources: Big Four firm websites and The Lawyer)

That would be a mistake. Large law firms are getting larger, but mergers that are driven by well-conceived strategy appear to be outnumbered by those driven by at least one of the firms being in distress. Premium work is concentrating in law firms with the best talent and competitive value propositions, of which price is but one facet.

Law firms that deliver services that can be technologically codified and digitally delivered with minimal human input are especially at risk. Traditionally, observers have automatically lumped mid-sized firms into this category. Depending on their ability to embrace digital transformation, though, some of those firms may be better placed than larger competitors to thrive in the market that is emerging. For premium law firms, attracting and retaining the top-tier talent required to leverage the work that the digital tools deliver is key to being able to deliver the new generation of legal services that will be of a sophistication that is rare, if not absent, in the market today.

Convergence

Very few changes are triggered by single drivers, acting in isolation of others. This applies very much to the digital drivers that are transforming global societies and economies. They act in complex, dynamic combination with each other and with geo-economic, socio-political and other trends. To a law firm, it makes sense to fixate on the impact

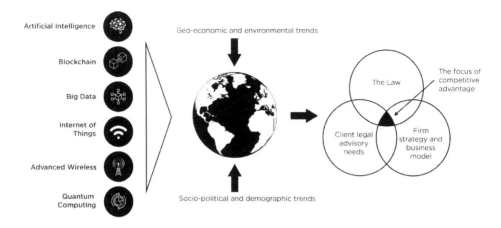

Figure 2: A thought model for thinking about the cumulative and dynamically interrelated impacts of multiple change drivers, in this case emerging disruptive digital innovations. These drivers act not in isolation but together with each other on society and markets, also in concert with geo-economic, environmental, socio-political and demographic trends. In turn, this impacts the law, client legal needs, and (hence) the business models of law firms. Competitive advantage can be found by focusing on the nexus of these three areas of impact. (© Cambridge Strategy Group)

that they might have directly on the structure and business model of the firm (for instance, by displacing much of the work currently done by paralegals and lawyers). Instead, one needs to consider the impact of these drivers on the law itself and on what new legal needs clients are likely to develop, and only then how those changes are going to impact the firm's strategy and its business model. This thought framework is illustrated in Figure 2.

The six digital drivers highlighted in the figure will drive radical change in the business models of law firms and other legal service providers, and also their clients. For those that seize the challenge and embark on the difficult task now of proactively evolving their business models, the promise includes a properly differentiated value proposition and higher profitability. For those who cling to the past, the future likely involves increased pressure as obsolescence of the old business model accelerates, eroding performance, flight of the firm's top performers to others offering better prospects, to eventually either a defensive merger or dissolution.

The six digital drivers are outlined below.

Artificial intelligence (AI)

The promise of artificial intelligence is a digital assistant who can almost instantaneously research every legal and other aspect of a complex matter

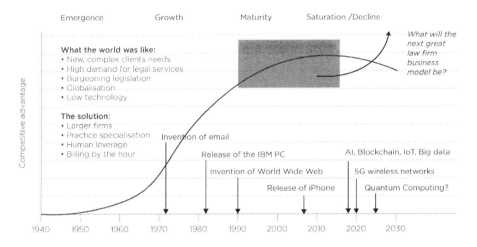

Figure 3: Like most trends, business models go through phases of emergence, rapid growth once they are accepted in the market, maturity as supply matches demand and then saturation or decline. The "Tournament of Lawyers" business model emerged in the early 20th century in response to disruptive technologies invented in the 19th century. The area shown in the grey block at the top of the 'S curve' is highlighted in figure 4

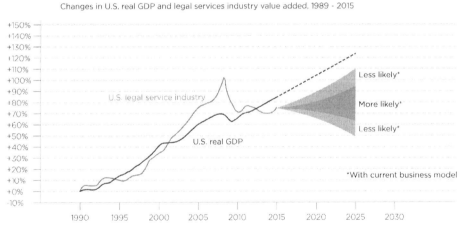

Figure 4: Growth in the contribution of US legal services tracked US GDP growth until the 1990s, then levelled off until the dotcom boom created additional demand, then accelerated to beyond GDP through the credit boom before correcting sharply in 2009/10. Since then, growth in legal services has stagnated. (Index with 1990 = baseline. Sources: IMF for GDP; US Department of Labor for legal services, which are defined by DoL as private law firms plus judiciary; CSG analysis)

and provide a lawyer with a good overview of a client's legal position. It promises to allow lawyers to elevate their advisory role from compliance, risk, and dispute resolution, to advising clients on how to use the law to improve their strategy and competitive advantage. Today, AI is limited to (increasingly sophisticated) machine learning applied to very narrow applications. With the advent of quantum computing, this is likely to explode into far more advanced applications, utterly transforming the role of lawyers and other advisors.

Blockchain

By removing the need for intermediaries, blockchain technologies are poised to transform both those who act as intermediaries (financial institutions, agents and many kinds of advisors – including some kinds of legal advisory work) and the industries that depend on them (almost every kind of industry, hence law firm clients). Most of the attention and hype today is focused on cryptocurrencies. The immutability, transparency, privacy, and efficiency that underpin blockchains are likely to be even more transformational to client businesses and legal needs, though, hence also to law firm business models. They might even fundamentally impact the rule of law by controlling, through technology, many aspects of life where behavior is governed by law but compliance mechanisms are poor.

Big data

At least a dozen definitions of big data are in circulation. The *Oxford English Dictionary* defines it as: "data of a very large size, typically to the extent that its manipulation and management present significant logistical challenges".

Thinking of "big data" as simply requiring very large storage devices does not even begin to approach the reality of the concept. The amount of data being generated today is staggering. Much of it is irrelevant to needs such as discovery or due diligence, but how does one find the nuggets of value, lost in this vast sea of bits and bytes? This is where the intersection with AI becomes important. Given sufficient computing power, AI can scan vast tracts of data and distil it down to quantities that can be managed by humans. As an added benefit, the relevant content is then far more concentrated so the work less mind-numbing.

Just how vast is "big data" potentially? By the end of 2017, roughly 1/20th of a Yottabyte (a Yottabyte being 1024 bytes) of electronic data existed on earth. If stored on standard 4.7GB DVDs, a stack of DVDs that contained a Yottabyte of data would extend 2.3 times the distance from the earth to the sun. Clearly, in a world of Yottabytes of data, and beyond, we cannot still be thinking about rooms of files and papers and associates trawling through documents in the same way as before.

Internet of Things

The Internet of things (IoT) is the network of objects (including physical devices, vehicles, and home and industrial appliances) that are connected with each other via the internet. These are able to exchange data and trigger actions, not necessarily with human intervention. In 2017, 8.4 billion online devices were connected through the IoT, expected to reach 30 billion by 2020. The global market value of the IoT is expected to reach $7.1 trillion by 2020.

So far, the IoT has consisted mostly of devices exchanging small amounts of data and triggering only limited actions. The advent of 5G and later, future generations of wireless networks, will allow greater exchanges of data. Blockchain will allow smart contracts to be embedded in the IoT, even linked to AI enabled devices. Interesting legal questions will result around liability, should IoT devices trigger acts that were not anticipated by their owners or developers. Lawyers are likely to require sophisticated digital tools (as yet not invented) to unravel the tangle of contractual liability, tort, and redress involved in the disputes that will inevitably follow.

5G and further wireless network advances

Following its debut at the 2018 Winter Olympics at Pyeongchang, South Korea, 5G technology is now well proven. It is poised to be commercially deployed by about 2020 and promises:

- Download speeds of 10Gbps (which is ~100x faster than 2017);
- To connect seven trillion wireless devices serving seven billion people;
- Zero perceived downtime;
- 90 percent reduced energy needs through new efficient micro base station technology; and
- Cost per unit of data transmitted falling at the same rate that data volume increases.

Convergent with the IoT and machine learning and blockchain, 5G will start to unlock the potential of autonomous vehicles. High quality broadband being accessible in remote rural communities, coupled with advances in localized electricity generation and quality online education platforms, could transform the lives of those living in frontier communities. It will enable knowledge workers (especially) to live and work away from cities if they so choose.

Further generations of advanced wireless networks will likely include a lattice of geostationary satellites delivering high definition mobile multimedia communication and ultra-high-speed data streaming, anytime anywhere. Clients will be able to expand into areas where poor connectivity currently prevents that. Lawyers will need to find ways of following them.

On the other hand, history has taught us that data flows tend to grow in step with the increased bandwidth available. It is entirely possible that in years to come we will still be complaining about buffering and connection failures caused by overload from a proliferation of IoT devices and far more data-intense applications such as entirely new forms of media and augmented reality.

Quantum computing

The principles of quantum mechanics are unfamiliar even to most scientifically literate people. The notation is different and the mathematics complex. The concept of quantum computing itself, however, is not new. Nobel Prize winning physicist, Richard Feynman, was the first to realize, in the early 1980s, that computers might be possible that adopt a blend of classical states simultaneously, in the same way that matter does at subatomic levels.

Quantum computers already exist, but are in their infancy. IBM, Google, Lockheed Martin and others are racing to build the first market-ready machine. Professor Winfried Hensinger, a scientist at the University of Sussex in England, claimed in early 2017 to have developed "the first practical blueprint for a quantum computer capable of solving problems that could take billions of years for a classical computer to compute".

A properly scaled, fully functional quantum computer could have more computing power than all the computers in the world today, combined. It follows that the implications of a breakthrough, not only for law but for the global geopolitical balance of power, would be immense. The strategic implications of having access to quantum computers would be of a scale similar to that of having access to one of today's supercomputers, versus no computer at all. Some compare the quest for quantum computing to the "Manhattan Project" and the race to build the first atom bomb.

The sheer processing power of quantum computers will render existing cryptographic protocols obsolete. On the other hand, new cryptographic protocols will likely emerge that are probably impossible to even imagine with today's knowledge.

Coupled with AI and big data, one might easily imagine AI systems that trawl through unstructured data on a monumental scale uncovering trends and intelligence that are simply not discoverable even with today's most advanced AI.

Finding the way forward

The looming disruptions seem immensely complex and the future imponderable beyond the short- to medium-term. It follows that forecasting the impact of these technologies beyond that term is impossible. What does seem certain is that clients will seek sound legal advice in the future as they have in the past, but that the lawyers of the future will need to be considerably more digitally astute, to meet the challenge of the new kinds of legal needs that are already emerging as these trends unfold.

Business model transformation for legal services will likely be an evolutionary, incremental process iterated between law firms and their clients. Managing the transition will need balance between a strong sense of strategic direction and agility and resilience to constantly fine-tune when things change. Constructive steps that law firm leaders can take, to make the transition easier, include the following.

Develop a digital culture

Ensuring that the conversations in the firm about emerging technologies are constructive. Recently, I learned of two prominent London law firms who were omitted from an invitation to pitch for technology-related legal work, because of comments by members of those firms in posts on social media. These were taken to be evidence of a lack of progressive thinking about emergent technologies and the challenges that the client faces. Ironically, both those firms would regard themselves as technologically astute. Impressions, it turns out, can be fragile.

Using some of the emerging AI and other tools and making sure that everybody in the firm is aware of it, and successes achieved, is another obvious way to develop a digital culture. Incorporating a digital "look and feel" to the firm's branding is yet another. Most of all, though, the everyday conversation within the firm needs to routinely include emerging client needs and how lawyers might use digital innovations to enhance the quality of the work they do. New information emerges all the time, so that conversation needs to be ongoing.

Leverage the wisdom of crowds

It is well accepted that solutions to poorly defined, obtuse problems that are derived from polling a broad base of knowledgeable people are usually better than those developed by a small group of experts. In law firms, the success of a solution is frequently as dependent on its acceptance by the firm's people, than on its technical correctness – especially where it is not going to be easy or comfortable to implement. Involving a broad base of the firm's people in developing that solution can significantly enhance the chances of its acceptance.

Proactively engage with clients about their future legal needs

Clients are at least as worried as law firms about the likely impact of disruptive technologies on their businesses. Many are unclear about how their business risks and legal needs will change. They are looking to their law firms to advise them on this, frequently not as paid engagements but as mutual investments in the future relationship. Speaking at a workshop on AI, blockchain, and legal services at MIT in late 2017, a senior leader of a prominent US law firm called the opportunity to work with clients to discover their emerging legal needs, as collaborative explorations, "the most promising business development opportunity that law firms have had in years."

Start work now on developing the new suite of services and service delivery channels

All areas of legal practice will be radically changed as digital disruptions gather momentum, and in different ways for clients across different industry sectors. Once your lawyers have developed enough insight into how client needs are likely to evolve, they will be in a position to assess how your firm's current suite of services need to evolve in response. Similarly, they will be able to assess how competitive the current service delivery channels will be and what opportunities exist to radically transform them – rather than just seek to make them more efficient within our current, primarily people-leveraged business models. Obviously, it makes no sense to develop a suite of services for which clients are not yet ready, but being at the forefront of innovation, during periods of great change, frequently yields dividends that are absent when markets are more constant.

Exchange ideas with the LegalTech community and others with diverse perspectives

Technology has traditionally been relegated to business support services in law firms – a means of supporting the practice, rather than as an integral part of the practice. This will certainly change as digital leverage gains ground. Again, the process is likely to be incremental and iterative. The LegalTech community is keen to learn from lawyers, to help focus the products they develop. Progressive lawyers are keen to find technology that really works – before competitors do. Much scope exists for synergistic collaboration. When diverse groups are brought together to discuss complex issues, far more innovative solutions emerge than if the group is uniform. Allen & Overy's "Fusion" project is a good example of this, where technology companies occupy space within the law firm and opportunities are actively explored together. So too the range of workshops and design-thinking sessions that some firms host, in search of the insights they need. Participation in hackathons like the "Global Legal Hackathon" can also infuse a high intensity burst of multi-disciplinary creative thinking.

Billing practices

The billable hour will probably always be necessary for some kinds of work. In the people-leveraged, "Tournament of Lawyers" business model, it is likely to be less prevalent. Digital tools like AI machine learning are currently regarded as tools to aid lawyers in being more productive and valuable to clients. Their cost is an overhead. This model breaks down as investments in digital tools increase and the tools themselves become units of production. The architectural and engineering professions are good examples of where this transition has already occurred, with the most complex and difficult work being done by CAD, working together with and controlled by skilled professionals. Making wider use of alternative billing structures now will make it easier when the digitally-enabled business model forces them to become the norm.

Multidisciplinary work

Work built on the output of emerging digital legal analytical tools will likely interface far more with other disciplines than legal work has before. This aligns well also with pressures from clients, that lawyers evolve from being focused primarily on advising on compliance, risk, and dispute resolution. To clients, these have become lower value roles. The higher value roles involve advising on the implications of law for their business strategy and competitive advantage in their markets. Lawyers might find that the areas where legal issues need to be tackled in isolation of other disciplines will decrease. Multi-disciplinary practices would be at an advantage and, indeed, the Big Four have this at the core of their value proposition. Law firms in jurisdictions where collaboration is restricted between lawyers and "non-lawyers" (a term that will have no place in the digital law firm of the future) will likely find themselves increasing at a disadvantage to firms not so hamstrung, and unable to deliver the level of service that their clients require.

In summary

Disruption is transformation that one doesn't see coming. The indicators of what digital transformation will mean for law firms are now well established. The basic characteristics of the business model of the digital law firm of the future is becoming apparent. Law firms are not hampered by vast legacy investments in equipment and factories that have become obsolete. To transform, they have only to change the way people think and their skills and competencies. Investment will be needed in new digital platforms and other new systems and processes, but funding that can easily be built into financial models that fit the needs of partnerships, with minor modifications. The demand for legal services is unlikely to end, anytime soon.

In 10 years, many of the law firms that lead the market today will almost certainly still exist and be thriving, but with radically different business models. Many other firms will have disappeared, and new names will also be amongst the leaders. The destiny of your firm is likely a matter largely of decisive choice, strong leadership, and the determination of your partners to do what needs to be done.

Chapter 11:
AI on the ground – the voice of the legal profession

By ARK Group

It is clear from this publication alone (not to mention the many hundreds of articles amassing daily on the benefits of AI in the legal space) that the law profession is undergoing rapid change with the influx of new technology. Whether you remain convinced that AI is a fad – an expensive waste of money that won't ever replace the role of human lawyers – or are now firmly in the camp that is creating use cases for AI technology with an eye on rapidly increasing personnel costs, the fact is, AI and intelligent computing capacity is greatly affecting the legal profession, and will ultimately change the way in which traditional law firms operate.

As this title was going to press, a February 2018 study by LawGeex[1] was published. In this landmark study, 20 US lawyers with decades of experience in corporate law and contract review were pitted against the LawGeex AI algorithm to spot legal issues in five Non-Disclosure Agreements (NDAs), totalling 11 A4 pages, containing 30 different legal issues.

The lawyers competed against a LawGeex AI system that has been developed for three years and trained on tens of thousands of contracts. The research was conducted with input from academics, data scientists, and legal and machine-learning experts, and was overseen by an independent consultant and lawyer.

The lawyers achieved an average 85 percent accuracy rate. The AI achieved 94 percent. The 20 lawyers took on average 92 minutes to complete the task. The AI took 26 seconds.

Critics will argue that AI technology will never fully replace humans, as if a firm wishes to have 100 percent accuracy in its contract review procedures, humans will be needed to check the computer's work. However, plaudits point out that the greatly reduced time the machine takes to review the tasks (in this case, the AI was over 100 times quicker than the fastest lawyer), coupled with the fact that it requires no downtime, and will not be distracted from the task at hand with more pressing matters, will mean there is definitely an argument for thoughtful consideration of the technology.

Whilst collecting the insights featured in this book, and the interesting and thought-provoking use cases that are contained within, we also carried out a survey of our global readership as to their use of AI within the legal profession. Respondents came from across the world, from such diverse law firms as Jackson Walker, Dentons, Foley Hoag, Goulston and Storrs, Cooley and Winston & Strawn LLP, and all had differing job roles within these firms, from research attorneys to librarians, business development professionals to directors of information services. We were keen to discover what those "on the ground" are thinking and feeling about the application of AI, and how they could envisage that changing in the future.

First, we asked if respondents were currently using any AI or robotics technology in their firms. Results were pretty evenly mixed, with 62 percent saying yes, and 38 percent saying no, or not yet. The areas in which they were using it differed, from contract review (30 percent), legal research (22 percent), intelligent interfaces (four percent), and e-discovery (eight percent). This tallies with the way the AI market is being led, with contract review vendors far outweighing other services, to date. However, with consultancy firm, McKinsey, estimating that 22 percent of a lawyer's job and 35 percent of a paralegal's job can be automated, these areas may get broader.

Of those who said they weren't using AI technologies currently, 33 percent intended to start within three to 12 months, 22 percent within 12 to 18 months, and 39 percent within 18 months to five years, with just six percent saying they were not planning on using it at all.

We then asked which program and/or vendor they were using. Unsurprisingly, most of the big names (most of which are featured in this book) came up, such as Kira Systems, Luminance, eBrevia, ROSS Intelligence, IBM Watson, as well as Contract Express from Thomson Reuters, and iManage RAVN. Of course, there are many other vendors available and it is not the intention of this publication to act as a marketing agent; that said, there are evidently some key players leading the way.

We were interested to establish what impact our respondents thought AI would have on legal services. A sizable 48 percent believe it will revolutionise legal services delivery, with an equal number predicting it will replace some jobs at lower levels in law firms. Four percent maintained it was just hype. Others commented:

"It may force departments, individuals, and organizations to take a more proactive approach to re-evaluating how they do things to leverage AI in improving efficiency. It may also prompt people and departments to have to analyze how they can adapt or evolve to continue staying relevant to their organization."

"It will not replace lawyers but augment lawyers and other professional staff, creating opportunities for allied professionals to provide more value to clients."

"It will allow the firm to focus on more value-added tasks for our clients and reduce the mundane workload."

With this question in mind, we asked if respondents were concerned about the impact of AI. Fifty-two percent said yes. One respondent said it wasn't so much the impact of AI, as its perception:

"People tend to be afraid of it. They don't realize they are already using AI in their personal lives. They don't know what it means to their jobs. We have to talk about AI differently than other software/technologies."

Corroborating this, one respondent simply said "SkyNet"; however, taking a more serious tone, another said there was "too much trust and not enough oversight", whilst another warned that, "Absent a concrete business need, 'solutions in search of a problem' become significant distractions for decision makers that draw resources away from more tangible, impactful initiatives".

On a different note, one respondent foresees that "Slow adoption by some firms will lead to a large gap in capability for late adopters versus those with large IT/data investment strategies", and indeed, it seems those law firms with larger budgets are the ones who will gain advantages in the short-term.

Cost is one of the major limiting factors blocking the use and uptake of AI. Fifty-eight percent perceive cost to be a major blocker, only narrowly exceeded by public perception (62 percent), with widespread concerns about lawyer resistance and "myopic" vision from Management that will stifle spending on AI due to other budget priorities. Thirty-eight percent believe the technology is not yet ready, and the extra time and effort it will take to train staff to use it is too much of a burden.

Despite this bleak outlook, respondents were fairly unanimous in their opinions as to the challenges that AI will help overcome. Internal efficiency gains scored the highest, with 78 percent agreeing the technology will make processes quicker, more efficient, and less labour-intensive, as can be demonstrated by all of the case studies featured in this publication. In close second, and closely related, was reducing costs, with 74 percent predicting a favorable return on investment in AI. Fifty-two percent agreed AI would help improve associate retention due to a reduction in dull process work, whilst 41 percent thought AI could become an alternative for those who cannot access or afford lawyers, again as has been demonstrated earlier.

Finally, we asked respondents for their thoughts on how the blockchain might affect legal services. A surprising 52 percent were looking into the subject, describing it variously as:

- Another innovation lever to increase efficiency and knowledge sharing;
- Having the potential to change the way legal services are delivered, how governments interact with citizens and how financial systems interact with customers; and
- Impacting security and taking control away from the lawyers.

Overall, the future for the law profession certainly seems to include AI, in some form or scope. Whilst it may still be early days, we are increasingly seeing law firms looking to adapt the ways in which they work to make room for the technology once it is ready, and it is likely these will be the firms that hit the ground running when it does.

Reference

1. www.lawgeex.com/AIvsLawyer